COMPLETE

PRELIMINARY
for Schools

Workbook
without answers

B1

WITH AUDIO
DOWNLOAD

Caroline Cooke

Cambridge University Press
www.cambridge.org/elt

Cambridge Assessment English
www.cambridgeenglish.org

Information on this title: www.cambridge.org/9781108539111

© Cambridge University Press & Assessment and UCLES 2019

First published 2019

20 19 18 17 16

Printed in Dubai by Oriental Press

A catalogue record for this publication is available from the British Library

ISBN 978-1-108-53911-1 Workbook without answers with Audio Download

Contents

Vocabulary extra

1 My life and home

1 Put the letters in order to make words for objects you can find in a house.

1 I don't have a *evdut* on my bed in the summer. It's too hot. ....

2 I only use one *olwilp* when I am sleeping. ....

3 Put the dirty plates in the *kins* and I'll wash them later. ....

4 Don't forget to put the milk back in the *drfeig*. ....

5 We often make popcorn in the *vwiromace* before we watch a film at home. ....

6 Have you got a *elwot* I can use to dry my hands? ....

7 I looked in the *rorimr* to see if I had chocolate on my face. ....

8 I turned on the hot *pta* but the water was cold! ....

2 Complete the sentences with *in*, *on* or *at*.

1 I'll see you .... six o'clock outside the cinema.

2 I love to go walking .... spring when it's not too hot.

3 You'll find the toilets down the corridor .... the right.

4 We went to play baseball .... the park.

5 I arrived late .... the evening after swimming practice.

6 I left my bus pass .... home, so I had to walk into town.

7 There's a clock .... the wall in the kitchen.

8 Lola usually eats with her family .... her birthday.

Countable and uncountable nouns

3 Put the words in the correct column.

> beach   bus   cooker   day   electricity   floor   food
> friend   furniture   game   hall   homework   house
> make-up   money   rain   shampoo   space
> tap   time

Countable	Uncountable

Reading Part 5

CIRCUS LIFE

Saran is an acrobat. She works in a circus that travels around the world. What is unusual is that she is eleven years old and already a full-time circus performer. Her daily **(1)** .... is actually quite strict. Most days she gets up late and **(2)** .... maths, science and English classes with the rest of the children in the circus. Then she trains for two hours every afternoon before the **(3)** .... in the evening. Normally, Saran, like all of the other members of the circus, does five or six performances a week, so it's **(4)** .... work. Her parents are also part of the circus and make sure Saran gets enough sleep and has a healthy **(5)** .... Although she doesn't have many hours of school, she speaks four languages and has been to many countries, so her **(6)** .... of the world is greater than most children her age.

1 For each question, choose the correct answer.

1 **A** way	**B** custom	**C** routine	**D** habit
2 **A** attends	**B** makes	**C** sits	**D** goes
3 **A** play	**B** exhibition	**C** presentation	**D** show
4 **A** heavy	**B** hard	**C** huge	**D** long
5 **A** food	**B** dish	**C** diet	**D** supply
6 **A** advice	**B** knowledge	**C** education	**D** information

Listening Part 2

 1 02 For each question, choose the correct answer.

1 You will hear a boy and his mother talking about his school books.
What do they decide to do with his books?
A put them away in his bedroom
B lend them to someone else
C throw them away

2 You will hear a boy telling his friend about helping at home. How does he feel about it?
A excited by the idea
B annoyed that his brother doesn't help
C confident that it won't take long

3 You will hear two friends talking about a trip.
The boy says he will miss the trip because
A he's going away with his parents.
B he hasn't got the right equipment.
C he has made a mistake with the date.

4 You will hear two friends talking about a TV series.
What does the boy like about the series?
A It shows realistic teenage situations.
B It has good actors.
C It had a surprising ending.

5 You will hear two friends talking about a house.
What is the problem with the girl's new house?
A It's too far from her school.
B She has to share a bedroom with her sister.
C It's dangerous to cycle outside it.

6 You will hear two friends talking about a new video game. What is the girl's problem?
A She hasn't got a castle.
B She can't cross the river.
C She's got too many gold coins.

Grammar
Frequency adverbs

1 Put the words in order to make sentences.

1 a / I / good / day / every / breakfast / eat

....

2 take / days / dog / I / the / park / to / my / most

....

3 in / eat / They / restaurant / a / occasionally

....

4 year / go / once / I / skiing / a

....

5 questions / She / ask / often / class / doesn't / in

....

6 mornings / They / home / never / the / are / at / in

....

7 takes / hardly / on / He / holiday / photos / ever

....

8 every / Some / read / the / people / newspaper / day / almost

....

a few, a bit of, many, much, a lot of and lots of

2 Choose the correct option.

1 I'd like .... butter on my toast, please.

  A much   **B** a bit of   **C** a few

2 There aren't .... cushions in the living room.

  A few   **B** much   **C** many

3 Has your mother got .... friends from her childhood?

  A much   **B** lots   **C** many

4 Only .... people bought his record. It wasn't very popular.

  A a bit of   **B** many   **C** a few

5 I had to pay .... money for my new laptop.

  A a few   **B** a lot of   **C** much

6 My sister sings .... when she's in the shower.

  A a lot   **B** lots of   **C** much

7 I've got .... time if you want some help now.

  A lots of   **B** much   **C** a few

8 The children didn't have .... sugar on their cereal.

  A much   **B** many   **C** a few

Present simple and present continuous

3 Choose the correct option in *italics*.

1 We can't go out because it *snows / is snowing* today.
2 All the players *know / are knowing* that the match is tomorrow.
3 The supermarket *opens / is opening* at 10 o'clock on Sundays.
4 My sister *hates / is hating* TV programmes about history.
5 Oliver often *misses / is missing* the bus on Monday mornings.
6 Most police officers *wear / are wearing* a uniform for work.
7 My little brother *grows / is growing* very quickly this year.
8 My mum *learns / is learning* Japanese at the moment.
9 The weather *gets / is getting* better this month.
10 Some people *watch / are watching* too much TV.

4 Complete the letter with the correct form of the verbs in brackets.

Hi Roberto,

I'm very happy we are penfriends. Here is some information about me. I (1) .... (live) in Sofia, the capital of Bulgaria, with my parents and my brother. I (2) .... (have) a dog and I often (3) .... (go) for walks with him to one of the beautiful parks near my house. Today it (4) .... (rain) so I can't go out and my dog (5) .... (sit) watching TV with me. He (6) .... (love) cartoons but he (7) .... (not enjoy) films! I (8) .... (go) to school far from my house, so every day I (9) .... (catch) the bus at 8 o'clock. This year I (10) .... (need) to pass some important exams so I (11) .... (study) hard at the moment, but I occasionally (12) .... (see) my friends at the weekend. We really (13) .... (like) playing video games together and we usually (14) .... (meet) at my house. What (15) .... (you / do) at weekends?

Write soon!

Best wishes,

Daniela

Writing Part 1

- Remember there are four points you have to answer in the email. Make sure you answer each one and add enough information about each point so that your email is about 100 words. Use words like *because, so* or *and*.

- You can use questions to make suggestions, give invitations or ask for further information.

1 Match the beginnings and endings of the sentences.

1 Let's meet at 10 o'clock
2 Wednesday is the best day
3 The park is very big,
4 The beach is a great idea

a so we can cycle around the lake there.
b because I love swimming in the sea.
c because I don't have football training that afternoon.
d so we have time to buy some food first.

2 Complete the table with the questions.

Inviting

Suggesting

Asking for information

1 Would you like to come to my house?
2 Which is the best place to visit?
3 Shall we go to the park?
4 Do you want to meet my friends?
5 What kind of films do you like?
6 Why don't we have a picnic?

3 Read this email from your English-speaking friend Robin, and the notes you have made.

To:

From: Robin

Hi,

I'm writing with some great news. I'm going to stay at my uncle's house next summer for two weeks and he says I can invite a friend to come with me. Would you like to come and stay? — *Yes, thanks!*

Would you prefer to travel there by bus or by train? — *Say which and why*

The house is near the beach and the weather will be hot. What kind of activities should we do at the beach? — *Tell Robin*

We'll need some indoor activities to do in the evenings. I'll bring some magazines for us to read. What else should we bring with us? — *Offer to take*

Lots of love,

Robin

Write your email to Robin using all the notes.
Write about 100 words.

Vocabulary

fail, pass, take, lose, miss, study and *teach*

1 Complete the sentences with a word from the box.

> do   fail   go   have x2   learn   lose   make   miss
> pass   pay   set off   study   take   teach   work

1 I have to .... for school at 7 o'clock because if I leave later, I'll .... the school bus.

2 In Year 13 we have to .... important national exams. If we .... them, we can go to university. I'm hoping to .... history.

3 Mr Brown likes to .... us new sports. This term we are going to .... how to play badminton.

4 I don't usually .... lunch at school. I prefer to .... home to eat.

5 If it's raining when we .... a break at school, we can stay in the classroom.

6 I can't find my bus pass. I hope I didn't .... it yesterday.

7 If you .... attention in class and .... notes while the teacher is talking, then you won't .... your exams.

8 In my school we often .... in groups and I usually .... my homework with a friend.

Reading Part 6

> • Read the whole text first before you complete any of the gaps.
>
> • The missing words are almost always 'grammatical' words, e.g. articles (*a, the*), auxiliary verbs (*have/has, is/was, do/does*), pronouns (*it, them, him, my*), prepositions (*in, at, for*) or linking words (*but, when, if*).

Exam advice

1 For each question, write the correct answer. Write one word for each gap.

THE BREAKFAST CLUB

Example: **0** of

Where do you have breakfast? I have mine at the canteen at school. There are usually loads **(0)** .... my friends there as well. There is plenty of choice, like cereal, toast or yogurt and we eat as much **(1)** .... we can.

Now I am older, I help with the breakfast club. There **(2)** .... some very young children who come at 7.30 in the morning and I look **(3)** .... two or three six-year-olds to make sure they eat well.

In my opinion, breakfast is the most important meal of the day because it helps my body and brain work better. If I have a good breakfast **(4)** .... day, I have more energy to study.

I love being **(5)** .... my friends and chatting in the canteen. After we have eaten, we clean the tables and we go to class, ready **(6)** .... start the day.

Grammar

Past simple

1 Complete the dialogues with the correct past simple form of the verbs in the box. You need to use some of the verbs more than once.

> do   earn   go   have   make   meet   spend   take

1 **A:** Yesterday I .... three hours doing those physics exercises for homework.

B: It .... me a long time, too. .... you .... the maths problems?

A: No, I .... (not) time.

2 **A:** My sister .... a music degree at university and now she plays in an orchestra.

B: .... she .... a lot of money when she started?

A: No, but she .... fun.

3 **A:** I .... to a summer camp last July.

B: .... you .... many friends?

A: Yes, I .... people from lots of different countries.

4 **A:** I .... (not) very well in the exam last week. I know I .... a lot of mistakes.

B: That's because you .... (not) much time revising.

A: I know. I thought I .... a good memory, but I was wrong!

Past simple, past continuous and *used to*

2 Choose the correct option in *italics*.

1 I *used to enjoy / was enjoying* history when I was in primary school but now it's very difficult.

2 He *gave / was giving* a presentation in the communication skills class when the computer *stopped / was stopping* working.

3 *Did you spend / Were you spending* a lot of money when you were on holiday last year?

4 It *was raining / used to rain* when we left the house but later the sun *came / was coming* out.

5 I *played / was playing* on my phone when I *received / was receiving* a text.

6 My parents *didn't use to let / weren't letting* me go out on school days.

7 The children *made / were making* so much noise in the playground that they *didn't hear / weren't hearing* the bell.

8 We *decided / were deciding* to have a cup of coffee while we *used to shop / were shopping* in the city centre.

3 Complete the text with the past simple or past continuous form of the verbs in brackets.

A terrible trip!

On the day of the school trip I **(1)** .... (wake up) as usual at 8 o'clock to go to school. I **(2)** .... (leave) the house when I realised I **(3)** .... (not have) my sandwiches, so I **(4)** .... (run) back inside. I **(5)** .... (set off) again and I **(6)** .... (walk) along the road when suddenly it **(7)** .... (start) to rain. At that moment, my friend Alice **(8)** .... (come) past in her mother's car and they **(9)** .... (stop) to pick me up. The excursion **(10)** .... (be) to the wildlife park about 15 minutes from our town. When we **(11)** .... (arrive) at school, the bus was waiting outside, so we **(12)** .... (get on) and sat down. Alice and I **(13)** .... (talk), so we **(14)** .... (not notice) the other students on the bus. Half an hour later we **(15)** .... (look) out of the window. We **(16)** .... (be) at the museum, not in the park! We looked at the other people around us and we **(17)** .... (see) they were from another class. It **(18)** .... (be) the wrong bus!

Listening Part 1

1 For each question, choose the correct answer.

03

1 What subject does the boy want to study at university?

A   B   C

2 Where is the girl's physics book?

A   B   C

3 When is the chemistry exam?

A   B   C

4 Which afterschool activity is most popular?

A   B   C

5 What did they do when it started to rain?

A   B   C

6 What was the first prize in the competition?

A   B   C

7 Why did the boy go to bed late?

A   B   C

Writing Part 2 (An article)

Exam advice

- Read the instructions carefully and check who you are writing the article for.
- Look at the title and the questions and think what sort of things you could write that would answer the questions in the exam task.

1 Read the task below. What information do you need to include in your answer?

You see this notice in an international English-language magazine.

> **Articles wanted!**
>
> **FUN ACTIVITIES AFTER SCHOOL**
> What's fun to do with your friends after school?
> Is it doing sport, doing something creative or learning a practical skill?
> How important is it to do something different from studying after school?
> **Write an article answering these questions and we will publish the most interesting articles in our magazine.**

Write your **article**.

2 Look at Charlie's ideas below. Tick (✓) the ideas that answer the questions in the writing task.

What's fun to do with your friends after school?	How important is it to do something different from studying after school?
1 You can go to the park and do some football training.	5 It's important to study a lot to pass your exams.
2 I have to do my homework, which is boring.	6 It's good for you to do something active after studying all day.
3 You can learn to play a musical instrument and start a band.	7 It's important to spend time with your friends outside of school to relax.
4 I go swimming every Tuesday with my dad.	8 I enjoy doing fun activities after school.

3 Make a list of your own ideas in the table below.

What's fun to do with your friends after school?	How important is it to do something different from studying after school?

4 Complete the sentences with a word from the box to make sentences for giving opinions.

> agree   opinion   sure   think

1 In my .... we should all have some time to do the things we enjoy.
2 I'm .... that exercise is really important for everyone.
3 I don't .... that we should do a lot of homework.
4 I .... it's a good idea to have a hobby.

5 Now write your answer to the task in Exercise 1 in about 100 words.

3 Having fun

> • Be careful with negative verb forms or words that have opposite meanings.
> • Check your answer by trying to work out what's wrong with the others.
>
> **Exam advice**

Jason talks about GEOCACHING

Geocaching is a great hobby, where you have to try to find hidden containers in the countryside from information that's posted on the internet by other people. Using an app with a map, you can find the location and race your friends to be the first one there and open the container. It's surprising what people leave inside and there are some hiding places that I would never have thought of.

My initial experience with geocaching was quite an adventure. My whole group was new to the activity, so it wasn't the best-planned trip. The first problem was with technology. My phone didn't have enough memory to download the app, so I ended up having to share with a friend. This meant that either we had to go at the same speed or one of us got left behind and wasn't able to join in. That one was often me when I felt tired.

Since then, I have become quite a fan and I even create my own geocaches, where I put objects such as badges, sweets or even sometimes money, for others to find. There's a real community of people who are into playing. They have set up clubs to get together to play and then go for a meal afterwards. There are numerous blogs about the best gifts to replace anything you take or where there might be a new geocache. You might wonder what the farmers and others who live in the countryside think about this invasion of hunters but in general they seem quite happy as long as the visitors respect the environment and their privacy.

So, if you want to try something new and get out in the fresh air, call a few friends and take them for a day's hunting. It's perfect for families with children, especially those who protest when their parents try to get them off their screens and outside. The motivation of going from one hiding place to another as fast as possible means they walk a long way without realising, and even enjoy spending time with their parents!

1 Read the text. For each question, choose the correct answer.

1 Jason thinks geocaching
- **A** helps people to use technology.
- **B** takes a long time to arrange.
- **C** shows people have a lot of imagination.
- **D** prepares people for races.

2 Jason says the first time he went geocaching
- **A** he had difficulties remembering where to go.
- **B** he forgot to take some essential equipment.
- **C** the people he went with were more experienced than he was.
- **D** he couldn't participate as much as he wanted to.

3 Geocache players
- **A** need to be very organised.
- **B** exchange ideas about the game.
- **C** often live in the countryside.
- **D** want to protect nature.

4 Jason suggests that geocaching
- **A** is good for relationships.
- **B** is best for small groups of people.
- **C** doesn't work well in the city.
- **D** isn't suitable for lazy people.

5 What might Jason say to a friend who wants to try geocaching?
- **A** You'll need a good map and be careful of people who don't like you to walk on their land.
- **B** Make sure you have the right equipment and don't forget to bring some gifts to put in the boxes.
- **C** It's important to win and you'll get some amazing prizes if you are able to find the right locations.
- **D** If you don't like walking, you'll find this boring but you can always chat to your friends online and eat good food.

Vocabulary

Prepositions of place

1 Look at the picture and complete the sentences with a preposition.

1 The coach is standing .... the notice board.

2 There is a clock .... the wall.

3 The clock is .... the poster.

4 The shelves are .... the right of the notice board.

5 The photo is .... the cups.

6 The basketballs are .... the door.

7 The rackets are .... the helmets.

8 There are some trainers .... the corner.

Phrasal verbs

2 Replace the words in bold with a phrasal verb from the box in the correct form.

> give up   go on   hang on   join in   look after
> run out of   set off   sign up

1 We **had no more** milk, so I went to the supermarket. ....

2 If you want to **put your name down** for the course, you have to go online. ....

3 Can you **wait** a minute? I'm nearly ready. ....

4 Would you like to **be part of** the game? We need another player. ....

5 I decided to **stop** playing tennis because I hurt my arm. ....

6 We **left home** at 6 o'clock to get to the airport at 7.30. ....

7 Do you want to **continue** working or shall we have a break? ....

8 Can you **take care of** my fish when I go on holiday? ....

People's hobbies

3 Choose the correct option in *italics* and complete the sentences with the person who has the hobby.

1 A person who *rides / plays* a bicycle is called a ....

2 A person who *plays / does* chess is called a ....

3 A person who *makes / takes* photographs is called a ....

4 A person who *goes / plays* diving is called a ....

5 A person who *plays / touches* a musical instrument is called a ....

3

Exam advice

- You will hear the answers to the questions in the same order as the questions. If you don't hear the information for one question, move on to the next. You will have the opportunity to listen for a second time.

- It's important to choose an answer, even if you aren't sure.

1 For each question, choose the correct answer.

You will hear a radio interview with a young magician called Megan.

1 Megan decided to become a magician
  A when she saw a magician perform.
  B because her friends encouraged her.
  C after she joined a magician's club.

2 At the magic club, Megan
  A didn't get to perform many new tricks.
  B wasn't a typical member of the group.
  C didn't come first in a competition.

3 What does Megan say about her work in an office?
  A She had to study hard to get her job.
  B She doesn't mind not earning much money.
  C She doesn't have time to do much magic.

4 What does Megan say about the magic she performs?
  A She talks very fast while she does her tricks.
  B She uses a lot of movements.
  C She doesn't use any sounds.

5 What did Megan's mother think about her magic?
  A She enjoyed watching her daughter practise magic tricks.
  B She wanted her to improve as a magician.
  C She thought magic wasn't a proper job.

6 How does Megan feel about her life now?
  A pleased because she can do all the things she wants to
  B worried because she needs to make a decision
  C confident that she will be more successful in the future

Grammar

Verbs followed by *to* or *-ing*

1 Choose the correct option in *italics*.

1 I missed *to be / being* with my brother when he went to live abroad.
2 The students agreed *to meet / meeting* outside the station before they went to the party.
3 Brad hopes *to go / going* to university when he's older.
4 I learnt *to ride / riding* a bike when I was four.
5 Hannah doesn't feel like *to do / doing* much today because she's tired.
6 Have you finished *to read / reading* that book yet?
7 I don't mind *to see / seeing* that film again. It was excellent.
8 You should practise *to speak / speaking* in front of a mirror before you give your presentation.

2 Choose the correct sentence, a or b.

1 a Don't forget to wear your helmet when you're cycling!
  b Don't forget wearing your helmet when you're cycling!

2 a I remember my grandma to teach me how to make biscuits.
  b I remember my grandma teaching me how to make biscuits.

3 a Luckily I remembered putting on sun cream when I went sunbathing yesterday.
  b Luckily I remembered to put on sun cream when I went sunbathing yesterday.

4 a I'll never forget going diving in the sea for the first time!
  b I'll never forget to go diving in the sea for the first time!

3 Complete the conversation between three friends with the verb in brackets in the correct form: *to* + infinitive or *–ing*.

Katie: OK everyone. We need to finalise the plans for the trip this Saturday. What time shall we leave?

Ben: I suggest **(1)** .... (meet) at the youth club at 10 o'clock.

Katie: That's perfect. We'll have time to go shopping to get the food. Do you fancy **(2)** .... (eat) sandwiches? We can get some from the supermarket.

Ben: I can't afford **(3)** .... (buy) those. I think it'd be better to get bread and cheese to make our own sandwiches.

Katie: OK. Did you remember **(4)** .... (ask) your mum if we can borrow the picnic blanket?

Ben: Oh no, I'll send her a text now. I'm sure she'll say yes.

Katie: Liam, you promised **(5)** .... (bring) the map so we can plan the route.

Liam: Oh, I forgot **(6)** .... (put) it in my bag. I can run home and get it.

Katie: Alright. We'll wait for you here and make a list of things we need to take. Do you remember **(7)** .... (go) on that trip last year when it rained and no one had a raincoat?

Ben: But we still enjoyed **(8)** .... (get) to the top of the mountain, didn't we? Do we *have* to be so organised?

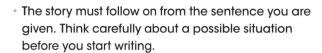

Writing Part 2 (A story)

- The story must follow on from the sentence you are given. Think carefully about a possible situation before you start writing.
- Don't change the sentence you are given.
- Plan your story. Make notes about what happens first, second, third, etc. before you start writing.

Exam advice

1 Read the exam task and answer the questions with your own ideas.

> Your English teacher has asked you to write a story. Your story must begin with this sentence.
> *I opened the door and was amazed by what I saw.*

1 Where was the door? In a house / hotel / school? In another place?
2 What did you see when you opened the door?
3 Why was it amazing?
4 What did you do?

2 Look at the beginning of two answers to this question. Which one follows the sentence in Exercise 1 better?

A I opened the door and was amazed by what I saw. The restaurant was full of people but they were all aliens! I closed the door and opened it again but they were all still there.

B I opened the door and was amazed by what I saw. My sister was sitting on the sofa and my dog was sleeping on the floor. I went into the living room and sat down to watch TV.

3 Write two or three sentences to continue the story that begins with this sentence. Use the questions below to help you.

I walked into the room and everyone stopped talking.

1 Where was the room?
2 Who was in the room?
3 Why did they stop talking?
4 What did you do?

4 Make notes about how the story continued. Use these ideas.

- What happened next?
- What did you say?
- What happened in the end?

5 Now write your story in about 100 words.

4 On holiday

Grammar

big and *enormous*

1 Choose the correct option in *italics*.

1 The water in the lake is absolutely *cold / freezing*.
2 Hiking all day in the mountains is *very / totally* exhausting.
3 We visited an *extremely / absolutely* fascinating sealife centre, which even had sharks.
4 The new earphones were *extremely / totally* small.
5 We gave the theme park a very *terrible / bad* review.
6 The weather was *quite / absolutely* boiling in the desert.

Comparative and superlative adjectives, (*not*) *as … as*

2 Complete the sentences with the correct form of the adjective in brackets.

1 The .... (good) way to get to the island is by boat.
2 I prefer to walk because it's as .... (quick) as the bus.
3 Using Google maps is the .... (easy) way to get directions.
4 Why are you late? I expected you to be here .... (early).
5 Health and happiness are .... (important) than money.
6 In Moscow travelling by underground is .... (fast) than by bus.
7 That was the .... (bad) storm in ten years.
8 My suitcase was .... (heavy) after I put all my shoes in it.

a bit, a little, slightly, much, far, a lot

3 Complete the sentences with a word from the box and the correct form of the adjective in brackets.

> a bit   a little   a lot   as … as
> far   much   slightly   than

Sunshine Hotel
500€ a night 200 rooms
200 m from the beach
breakfast from 6-9 am
2 hours from airport

TIPTOP HOTEL
55€ a night 20 rooms
200 m from the beach
no breakfast available
20 mins from airport

The Grand Hotel
- 50€ a night
- 200 rooms
- 1 km from the beach
- breakfast from 9–11 am
- 15 mins from airport

1 The Tiptop Hotel is .... the Sunshine Hotel. (small)
2 The Sunshine Hotel is .... the Grand Hotel. (expensive)
3 The Sunshine Hotel is .... the Grand Hotel. (big)
4 It takes .... to get to the Tiptop Hotel from the airport .... to the Grand Hotel (long)
5 The Grand Hotel serves breakfast .... the Sunshine Hotel. (late)
6 The Tiptop Hotel is .... the beach .... the Grand Hotel. (near)
7 The Grand Hotel is .... the Tiptop Hotel. (cheap)
8 The Grand Hotel isn't .... the Tiptop Hotel. (small)

Reading Part 1

Exam advice

- Signs and short messages often have grammatical words missing. Think carefully about their complete meaning.
- Decide if any of the options are definitely wrong. Then look at the other two more carefully.

1 For each question, choose the correct answer.

1

WILDLIFE PARK

- **No swimming in the lake**
- **Barbecues allowed in the picnic area**
- **Take your rubbish home with you**

A You are allowed to swim in the water.

B You must throw things away in the park's rubbish bins.

C You can cook in a special place.

2

Hi Emily

Are you ready for the camping trip tomorrow? I've got a tent, but could you pack a torch? Mine's broken – I won't have time to replace it. Don't forget we're leaving early!

Kelly

Kelly wants Emily to

A remember to bring something for the trip.

B find something to use for cooking on the trip.

C leave something they don't need for the trip.

3

Hi Larry

I've got a problem with meeting on Friday. What about Saturday instead? There's a much better film on then. I hope you haven't got the tickets yet!

Ollie

A Ollie will buy the tickets for the cinema.

B Ollie wants to go to the cinema on a different day.

C Ollie is confirming that they will see the same film as previously planned.

4

ENTRY FREE FOR LOCAL RESIDENTS OR VISITORS UNDER EIGHTEEN OR OVER SIXTY-FIVE
IDENTIFICATION NECESSARY FOR ALL

A Everyone over eighteen has to pay to go in.

B If you live in the area, you can go in without paying.

C Certain people need to show a document for free entry.

5

Tessa

Have you tried that restaurant in the square next to the bank? I wouldn't go to the one near the bridge. The food can be expensive there, and it's not very tasty.

Jake

A Jake is recommending the food at the restaurant near the bridge.

B Jake is telling Tessa to try the food in several restaurants.

C Jake is suggesting it's cheaper to go to the restaurant in the square.

Vocabulary

Buildings and places

1 Match the places with the signs.

1 art gallery
2 department store
3 fountain
4 library
5 sports centre
6 youth club
7 town hall
8 stadium

a
Don't throw rubbish in the water

b
TEMPORARY EXHIBITION – *Landscapes from the 18th century*

c
LIFT TO SECOND FLOOR – CHILDREN'S CLOTHES

d
ADVENTURE AND COMIC BOOKS

e
Friday night fancy-dress party. Under-eighteens only

f
Lions vs Bears *Champions match – tickets here*

g
Council meeting here Friday 8.00 pm

h
Swimming classes 7–9 pm

Holiday activities

buy souvenirs   enjoy nature   go sightseeing
go snorkelling   make a fire   see animals
sleep in a tent   sunbathe

2 Complete the table with the activities. Some activities can go in more than one section.

wildlife holiday

camping trip

beach holiday

city break

travel, journey and trip

3 Choose the correct option in *italics*.

1 The *travel / journey / trip* from Paris to London only took two and a half hours.

2 Max is going on a *travel / journey / trip* to the mountains with his friends this Saturday.

3 How often do you *travel / journey / trip* abroad with your family?

4 Train *travel / journey / trip* is the most popular way to get around the country.

5 I hope you have a good *travel / journey / trip* tonight and arrive safely.

6 Erin has to go on lots of business *travels / journeys / trips* for her job.

Listening Part 3

- Use the headings in the notes to help you follow the recording.

- You only need to write one or two words. At the end, check you haven't written more. Check if the words should be singular or plural.

Exam advice

1 For each question, write the correct answer in the gap. Write one or two words or a number or a date or a time.

05

You will hear a guide talking about tours of a film studio.

OAKWOOD FILM STUDIOS
Maxie's Time Machine tour
The tour lasts: (1) ....
See the (2) .... that was Maxie's time machine.

The Totem Men tour
The tour lasts: 30 minutes
Visit (3) .... in the camp to learn about the daily life of the Native Americans.

Ricky Ranger tour
The tour lasts: 45 minutes
Learn how they made the (4) .... for the film.

Oakwood cafeteria and shop
Salads, burgers, pizzas. Closed on (5) ....
Buy souvenirs, such as (6) ....

Writing Part 1

Exam advice

- Connect your ideas using linking words, e.g. *since, as* and *although*.
- Try to use interesting vocabulary. Don't repeat words like *good* or *nice*.

1 Look at the exam task. Then tick (✓) the information (1–7) that the answer should include.

Read this email, from your English-speaking friend Toni, and the notes you have made.

To:

From: Toni

Hi,

Thanks for your letter. I wanted to tell you about my plans this summer. My family and I are going on holiday to your country in August. I'm really excited!

We'd like to visit some interesting places. Do you know a good place to go?

What is the place like?

We like sightseeing and being active. What can we do there that is fun?

Write soon,

Toni

Great!
Yes — say where it is.
Describe it.
Recommend . . .

Write your email to Toni using all the notes. Write about 100 words.

1 a comment about Toni's news ☐
2 the name and location of a place ☐
3 information about your last holiday ☐
4 a description of the place ☐
5 an invitation to visit your home ☐
6 a suggestion about an activity for a family to do together ☐
7 a suitable opening and ending ☐

2 Complete Talia's answer with the adjectives in the box. There may be more than one possibility.

amazing clean delicious excellent fascinating
historic long pretty tiny warm

Dear Toni,

I'm really happy you're visiting my country.

I think the best place to go is a village called L'Escala. It's on the coast near Girona, which is very close to the border between France and Spain. The village is very **(1)** .... and the coast is absolutely **(2)** .... There are lots of **(3)** .... restaurants and the food is **(4)** ....

You can go snorkelling there because the water is extremely **(5)** .... and there is a **(6)** .... beach where you can walk for hours. If you want to go sightseeing, there are some **(7)** .... places to visit or you can go shopping in the market on Sundays.

I hope you have a good holiday!

Love, Talia

3 Exam candidates often make mistakes with adjectives. Underline the mistakes in the sentences and correct them.

1 When we arrived at the top of the mountain we were absolutely tired.
2 We saw some fasinating sights on holiday.
3 It was amazed – the best experience of my life!
4 It's a very nice city with lots of historical buildings.
5 There was a beatiful view from the hotel balcony.
6 The rooms were a bit tiny but the food was delicious.

4 Write your own answer to the task in Exercise 1 in about 100 words. Use interesting adjectives.

5 Different feelings

Vocabulary
Feelings

1 Choose the correct option in *italics*.

1 The team was *cheerful / disappointed* when they lost the match by one point.
2 I was *jealous / embarrassed* when my brother got a new tennis racket and I didn't.
3 Isabelle never lends me anything, not even a pencil! She's so *serious / mean*.
4 Callum always sleeps with the light on, otherwise he feels *afraid / miserable* that something bad will happen.
5 I felt so *embarrassed / strange* when I forgot the words I had to say in the play.
6 I'm very *fond / bored* of my great-aunt Lily. She's so kind.
7 It was the first time I had to play the piano in public, so I was feeling *confident / nervous*.
8 Ethan felt *satisfied / ashamed* when his friend discovered he was lying.

2 Complete the sentences with an adjective from the box and a preposition. Sometimes more than one answer is possible.

> afraid angry ashamed bored crazy depressed pleased sure

1 Poppy was .... her sister when she borrowed her best dress without asking.
2 My cousin is .... spiders and runs away when he sees one.
3 We were .... watching TV all afternoon, so we turned it off and went to the park.
4 You should be .... your behaviour. It's terrible to upset someone like that!
5 Charlie's parents were .... him when he won first prize.
6 I don't enjoy football any more. I'm getting .... always being in the bottom team.
7 Are you .... the time the train leaves? Just check it again.
8 Jake is .... reggae music and listens to it all the time.

Adjectives and their opposites

3 Correct the adjectives in bold with an adjective from the box with the opposite meaning.

> complicated fantastic funny generous
> miserable ordinary positive relaxed

1 My brother is very **mean**. He always lets me borrow his things if I need them. ....
2 I was feeling **cheerful** because I missed the party and really wanted to go. ....
3 Josh was so **serious** that I couldn't stop laughing. ....
4 Jessie's instructions were so **simple** that I couldn't do the activity. ....
5 The film was absolutely **awful**. I can't wait to see it again! ....
6 I love Lucy. She has such a **negative** attitude to life, even when things go wrong. ....
7 Lydia is feeling **nervous** now that she's on holiday. ....
8 It was a very **strange** day – I got up, went to school, came home and went to bed, as usual. ....

Adjectives with -ed and -ing

4 Complete the sentences with the correct form of the words in brackets.

1 (bore)

  a The long train journey was ....

  b Sean was .... because he had nothing to do.

2 (embarrass)

  a It was really .... when I fell over in the street.

  b I felt .... because I wore the wrong clothes to the party.

3 (relax)

  a Sitting on the beach with a good book is ....

  b I feel .... when I listen to music.

4 (excite)

  a My friends are .... about the skiing trip.

  b The action film was really ....

5 (amuse)

  a Rachel laughed because the video clip was very ....

  b My grandfather was .... when he heard the joke.

Reading Part 4

- Decide which sentences are definitely wrong and then try to find evidence that shows why one of the remaining ones is right.

- Think about the grammar of the sentence. Do the pronouns in the options match the sentences before and after the gap – singular/plural, male/female, etc.?

Exam advice

1 Read the text about going to learn a language abroad. Did the writer enjoy the experience?

2 Five sentences have been removed from the text.
For each question, choose the correct answer. There are three extra sentences which you do not need to use.

Learning French in FRANCE

Finally the big day arrived. I was going on an exchange trip to stay with a French family. I was feeling nervous and excited because this was my first time on a plane and my first time travelling alone, without my parents. **(1)** .... We met Emily at the airport, a couple of hours before the flight.

The flight was fine, although it was strange seeing the city disappearing under me from so high up. The flight went by quickly because I was so busy chatting to Emily about our trip and how our different host families might be. During the flight, we decided that we shouldn't spend time together speaking in English during our month abroad. **(2)** .... Despite our agreement, I was worried that I wouldn't be able to say much the whole time I was in France. However, when my host family met me, I knew from the mother's warm smile that everything would be OK.

It was still a bit stressful at first, trying to understand and communicate, but after a couple of weeks it became easier. I spent a lot of time with the two teenagers in the family. **(3)** .... In fact, I learnt loads of interesting words from them, you know, the kind of things you don't find in books! I had one embarrassing moment when I used the wrong word when I was talking to their grandmother, but she was very relaxed about it. **(4)** ....

When the time came to say goodbye to my host family, I was very sad to leave. However, I have brought back some wonderful memories from this experience. The most important thing I've learnt is that if you're open and positive about learning a language, then it's much easier. **(5)** .... I've even started watching a television series in French and I'm surprised to find that I can understand a lot more than before my stay in France.

A   After all, you can't expect a language student to get everything right!

B   I've come back relaxed and much more confident in my ability.

C   I've paid attention to them and worked hard to do well.

D   Otherwise we wouldn't learn as much French.

E   I found it disappointing when I didn't understand.

F   They didn't have time to show me much.

G   Luckily, another girl from my class was going as well.

H   They were younger than me but we got on well.

Listening Part 2

1 **For each question, choose the correct answer.**

1 You will hear two friends talking about a sports centre. They agree that

    A the staff are welcoming.

    B the prices are reasonable.

    C it is well organised.

2 You will hear a girl talking to a friend about moving home.

How does she feel about it?

    A disappointed with the size of the house

    B pleased with the public transport in the area

    C worried about losing contact with her friends

3 You will hear a boy talking to a friend about a website. He thinks it is good because

    A students can use the photos on the site.

    B it has all the information they need.

    C it's easy to use.

4 You will hear a boy talking to his mother about a basketball match.

The boy is unhappy about the match because

    A he didn't play well.

    B he didn't play much.

    C his team didn't win.

5 You will hear a girl telling a friend about a board game.

She found it boring because

    A the other players knew more about the game than she did.

    B she had to wait a long time for her turn.

    C no one wanted to talk while they were playing.

6 You will hear two friends talking about a party.

The girl enjoyed the evening because

    A she got to know new people.

    B everyone was dancing.

    C she had an interesting conversation.

Grammar

can, could, might and may

1 **Choose the correct option in *italics*.**

1 When my grandad was younger, he *can / could* see very well but now he's old, he *can't / couldn't* read without glasses.

2 I'm not sure if I *can / may* finish this work today. I *can / might* have to do it tomorrow.

3 **A:** Where's Katie? I *can't / couldn't* find her.

    B: She *can / might* be in the playground. I saw her going in that direction a few minutes ago.

4 The football match *can / may* be cancelled because it *might not / might* snow this weekend.

5 **A:** *Can / May* you play the piano?

    B: No, but my brother *can / might* play very well.

Modals for advice, obligation and prohibition

2 **Choose the correct option in *italics*.**

1 You *shouldn't / don't have to* go to bed late when you have to get up early the next day.

2 You *mustn't / have to* lie to people if you want to stay friends with them.

3 You *shouldn't / have to* pay if you break something in a shop.

4 You *ought to / shouldn't* eat vegetables every day to be healthy.

5 You *should / don't have to* bring food for the trip. Lunch will be provided.

6 We *don't have to / must* turn off the lights when we're out, to save electricity.

Writing Part 2 (A story)

Exam advice

- Remember you should spend about 20 minutes writing your story. In this time you need to plan the story, write it and check it.

- Try not to repeat verbs and adjectives. Think of other words that mean the same but are more interesting.

- Don't write too many words over the limit – if you write too much, you are more likely to make mistakes.

1 Read the exam question. The words and phrases in the box show ideas you could use in this story. Put them into the correct part of the table.

> Your English teacher has asked you to write a story.
> Your story must begin with this sentence.
> *It was a day when everything went wrong.*

> angry   at school   miserable   on holiday
> I lost something   sad   my brother   nervous
> a teacher   a shop assistant   at home
> I forgot something   my family   depressed
> I missed the bus/train   a police officer   embarrassed
> a friend   disappointed   at a sports match
> I broke something

Place(s)	
People	
Problem(s)	
Feelings	

2 Read the answer below and number the events A–E in order. Ignore the gaps in the story.

- **A** I ran to the school.
- **B** I arrived at the sports centre.
- **C** All the other people thought I looked funny.
- **D** I called my friend.
- **E** I couldn't find my boot.

It was a day when everything went wrong. It was Saturday. I was feeling excited and **(1)** .... because I had an important match that morning. I went to the sports centre early, but it was empty. The man at the door said, 'There isn't a match here today.' I phoned my best friend. He was **(2)** .... and said, 'Where are you? The match starts in fifteen minutes.' Then, I remembered that the match was at school.

I ran as fast as I could. When I arrived, the teams were already playing. I went to change and saw that I only had one boot. I couldn't find the other one, so I went out to play with one boot and one shoe. Everyone laughed and I felt really **(3)** ....

3 Complete the story with interesting adjectives.

4 Now answer this exam task.

> Your English teacher has asked you to write a story.
> Your story must begin with this sentence.
> *It was the day I met my hero.*

Write your story in about 100 words. Think about the place, time, people and feelings.

Vocabulary
Television programmes

1 Match the sentences with the types of television programmes in the box.

> comedy series   cooking show   quiz show
> reality show   sports programme   the news
> wildlife documentary

1 Challenge yourself to answer the questions.
2 24-hour information about world issues.
3 You won't stop laughing.
4 Follow the progress of future chefs.
5 You'll find out about every detail of their lives.
6 The exploration of our oceans and the creatures that live there.
7 All the Champions League matches live.

Going out

2 Complete the text with the words in the box.

> admission   book   interval   live   perform
> refreshments   screen   stage   subtitles   tickets

Next week we have a complete range of events for all students at the college. On Wednesday evening there's a trip organised by the Music Club to see the Royal Opera Company **(1)** .... at the National Opera House. There are limited places on the coach, so **(2)** .... early if you want to go. For film lovers we are showing a series of short films from China on the big **(3)** .... in the Audio-visual department on Thursday night. The films will have **(4)** .... for those people who don't speak Chinese and **(5)** .... is free for all students with a student card. On Friday, our drama students will be on **(6)** .... in the Drama Club's performance of *Romeo and Juliet*. **(7)** .... will be provided in the **(8)** .... in the student café next to the main hall. And for fans of **(9)** .... music, join us for a special guitar concert in the café. You can get **(10)** .... for this event from the secretary's office on the first floor.

been/gone, meet, get to know, know and *find out*

3 Complete the dialogues with the correct verb in *italics*.

1 **A:** Have you *known* / *met* Michael for a long time?
  B: No, I only *knew* / *met* him last week.
2 **A:** What do you think of Lenny?
  B: I didn't like him at first, but now I've *got to know him* / *found him out* better, I think he's nice.
3 **A:** Where's Sean?
  B: I think he's *gone* / *been* home. He wasn't feeling well.
4 **A:** Hi, Tom. Where have you *gone* / *been*? I wanted to ask you something.
  B: Sorry, I had to talk to my tutor in the break.
5 **A:** Have you ever *been* / *gone* to a live concert?
  B: No, never, but I'd love to see a rock band.
6 **A:** Have you *found out* / *known* where we have to go tomorrow?
  B: No, the teacher hasn't told us yet.

Reading Part 2

1 The people below all want to watch TV tonight. Read the eight descriptions of TV programmes. Decide which programme would be the most suitable for each person.

1 Musa is spending the evening with friends from his sports club. They want to learn something useful and see a programme with plenty of action.

2 Sam would like to be a famous rock star one day. He loves listening to music from abroad and hearing new bands that aren't so famous. He isn't keen on competitions.

3 Aisha wants to watch a competition but she's bored with celebrities. She'd prefer to see something where normal people can take part.

4 Paveen is looking after her eight-year-old cousin Maya, who is crazy about animals. They both want to watch something funny and Maya's parents like her to watch educational programmes.

5 Danny loves watching series and he'd like to watch something that hasn't been on television before. He especially enjoys science-fiction shows that have famous actors in them.

Saturday NIGHT  TV GUIDE

A Celebrity Challenge
This great quiz show includes celebrity competitors who try to answer questions. Although these famous people come from the world of music or theatre, the questions are on any topic such as maths, sport or history. Test yourself as you watch. All you have to do is download the app and if you beat the rest, there are fantastic prizes.

B The Colony
Switch on to the first part of this exciting new thriller. It is set in a galaxy far away, where humans who escaped the destruction of Earth are now living. They learn to live with the aliens and deal with dangerous wildlife. It stars Oscar-winning actress, Tania Green. If you're interested in future worlds, this is one to watch.

C Sunny
This brand-new cartoon series follows the adventures of a group of penguins who play ice hockey. This sport takes them around the world to compete, and each week there is an original song performed by the polar bear fans. An amusing series that helps children learn about other cultures in an entertaining way, but older watchers will also enjoy it.

D Reporter Jack
This week Jack travels to the north of the country to meet a group of athletes training for the next World Games. They explain new training techniques for young people who want to succeed in field or track events. You can also see the most exciting moments in recent races.

E Star Time
The most popular weekly talent show on TV is now in its third season. Will a singer, a dancer or a gymnast win this week? From 6 to 60 years old, the performers have three minutes to give their best. They have often travelled from other countries to take part in the show.

F Universe
If you are a technology lover, then don't miss this special programme. We are all slightly scared about how much robots can control our lives, but here you will learn how they work and how we can control them. You can send a message to the experts and get instant on-screen answers.

G Saturday Escape
Imagine yourself skiing down a snowy mountain or parachuting from a plane. Well-known TV journalist Tiger Tom accepts a new challenge each week. This time it's bungee-jumping, and you can experience the jump moment by moment as he has a mini-camera attached to his helmet. Meanwhile his commentary about the experience will keep you laughing even though it's scary.

H Show Night Special
Continuing our events series, this week's programme brings you a live concert held to celebrate World Children's Day. Some well-known stars, as well as bands you've never seen before, will come together on stage. Musicians from over 30 countries will perform, and between songs they give tips on how to begin a career in music.

Grammar
Present perfect and past simple

1 Complete the sentences with a word from the box.

> already   for   just   since   yet

1 Oscar's been a successful actor .... six years.

2 I have to give the project in next week but I'm relaxed because I've .... done it.

3 The film has .... finished, so you can turn on your phone now.

4 She hasn't seen her uncle .... she was eight years old.

5 I haven't had any information about the exhibition .... I hope they'll send it tomorrow.

6 You don't need to call Danny. I've .... told him what time we have to be there.

7 Lorena's .... gone out. She left two minutes ago.

8 Have you received my email ....? The internet is so slow today.

2 Complete the sentences with the past simple or present perfect form of the verb in brackets.

1 How long .... (you / know) your best friend?

2 I .... (take) hundreds of photos on my last holiday.

3 I .... (not be) to the new stadium yet, but I want to go next week.

4 He .... (learn) to ride a bike when he was four.

5 I .... (tell) you three times already. Don't touch my computer!

6 We .... (go) to see a brilliant play last week.

3 Exam candidates often make mistakes with the present perfect and past simple. Underline the mistakes in the sentences and correct them.

1 I haven't see him since I was at school.

2 I lost my phone yesterday and haven't still found it!

3 Yesterday she's gone to Japan for two weeks.

4 I have wanted to learn to play the guitar since a long time.

5 I have bought my tablet five years ago but it still works really well.

6 We haven't seen that new film already.

Listening Part 1

- You will hear information about all three pictures. Listen to the complete conversation before you choose your answer.

Exam advice

1 For each question, choose the correct answer.

07   **1** Which programme did the boy enjoy?

   A   B   C

2 How much did the tickets cost?

   A   B   C

3 Where does the girl prefer to watch the football match?

   A   B   C

4 Which shirt does the boy buy?

   A   B   C

5 Who is the boy's history teacher?

A   B   C

6 What has the girl forgotten?

A   B   C

7 When did the concert finish?

A   B   C

Writing Part 2 (An article)

Exam advice

- Read the task and make notes to answer the questions. Use examples to explain your ideas and give your opinion.
- Use different paragraphs to write about each question.

1 You can use a question in an article to attract the reader's attention. Put the words in order to make questions.

1 ever / basketball / seen / Have / a / live / you / match / ?

....

2 people / Why / do / like / weekend / cinema / to / the / at / going / the / ?

....

3 you / going / Do / out / home / prefer / or / night / staying / Saturday / on / at / a / ?

....

2 Match the sentences A–C to the questions in Exercise 1.

A I enjoy both. It depends on how I feel.
B I think they enjoy the experience of seeing a film on the big screen.
C I went to the European Cup final and it was an amazing experience.

3 Read this exam task and the student's article below. Answer the questions.

1 What two forms of entertainment does the writer choose to write about?
2 What examples does the writer give?
3 What does the writer use to attract the reader's attention?

You see this announcement in an international English-language magazine for teenagers.

Articles wanted!
SATURDAY NIGHT ENTERTAINMENT
What's a good way to spend Saturday night?
Music? Film? TV shows? Sport?
Is it better to watch films at home or at the cinema? Why?
Write an article answering these questions and we will publish the most interesting articles in our magazine.

Write your article.

Is anything better than spending Saturday night with family or friends? My family and I often sit down together to watch a comedy show. We usually have dinner and then turn on the TV. I love it because the next day is Sunday, so I don't have to worry about homework.

Sometimes I like going out to the cinema, too. It's fantastic to see a good film on a big screen. The sound is better and you feel like you are part of the action.

If I have enough money, I prefer to go to the cinema to be with my friends and enjoy a special evening.

4 Write your own answer to the task in Exercise 3 in about 100 words. Try to include a question, an example and mention at least two of the types of entertainment given in the question.

7 Getting around

Exam advice

- Don't try to match words in the options with words in the text. Think about their meaning rather than the actual words.
- Check that the meaning of the option you think is correct exactly matches the information in the text.

1 For each question, choose the correct answer.

1

> I was sick all night, so I won't be able to go to school today. Can you email me today's homework? I hope Mrs Hill will let me do today's physics exam later!
>
> Rob

A Rob wants Lucy to do his homework for him.
B Rob has to go to school later because of the weather.
C Rob is worried because he will miss some important work at school.

2

To: Olivia
From: Ali

I'm sorry to hear about your broken arm. Our last match wasn't great. We needed you – you're our strongest player! Next week we're going to play at home. Come and see us!

Why has Ali sent Olivia this message?

A to see if Olivia will play with them next week
B to let Olivia know that she is important for her team
C to check if Olivia injured herself doing sport

3

BAGGAGE SALE

Wide range of light
hand luggage suitable for most airlines

•••

Cheap home delivery
for larger suitcases

A The shop will take the bigger suitcases to your house free of charge.
B The smaller cases aren't too heavy to carry.
C You can take the hand luggage on any plane.

4

Year 4 Students

Our internet connection isn't working because of the storm yesterday. Please bring a note signed by your parents for the school trip on Friday because we won't be able to receive emails until next week.

A Parents have to send an email next week to the school.
B Students must have permission in writing before they can go on the trip.
C The school trip has been cancelled because of a storm.

5

BIKES MUST BE LEFT IN THE AREA BEHIND THE GYM
NOT NEXT TO THE SCHOOL GATES

A You can't leave your bike near the entrance.
B You should bring your bike for PE class.
C You can't cycle in the area next to the school.

Vocabulary
Weather

1 Complete the sentences with a word from the box.

> foggy freezing frost ice rainy showers
> snowy sunshine thunderstorms windy

1 It's white outside this morning but it hasn't snowed. There's .... on the grass.

2 The rain started and stopped several times today. There were several ....

3 It was like driving through a cloud, so we had to go really slowly. It was very ....

4 It was so cold that the lake was frozen. You could see the fish under the ....

5 The temperature is below zero. It's ....

6 When there are .... , my dog is terrified by the noise and won't leave the house.

7 Take an umbrella in the .... season in Thailand because it can be very wet.

8 The main reason my parents go on holiday to the beach is to enjoy the ....

9 It's often very .... in that area near the sea, so it's popular with kite surfers.

10 I love it when the weather is .... and cold in the winter because we usually go skiing.

2 Exam candidates often make spelling mistakes. <u>Underline</u> the mistakes in the sentences and correct them.

1 The weather was suny and there weren't any clouds in the sky.

2 The temperture was about 30 degrees all week!

3 There was a terrible thuderstorm that lasted for ages.

4 During the day it's very hot but at night it's frezzing.

5 The wheather was great on Saturday so we went to the beach.

6 It was rainning a lot so I took my umbrella with me.

7 In the fogy weather the plane couldn't take off.

8 The tree was struck by lightening during the storm.

Compound words

3 Match the words in box A with the words in box B to make compound words. Then complete the sentences with the compound words.

A

> back camp cross guide over sight sign suit

B

> book cases night pack post roads seeing site

1 There is a .... at the .... showing the way.

2 The people want to do some .... , so they've got a .... to find the best places, but first they should leave their .... at the hotel!

3 We stayed .... at a .... I had to carry everything in my ....

7

Listening Part 4

> **Exam advice**
>
> • Don't worry if you're not sure of an answer the first time you listen. You will hear the recording again.
>
> • You may be able to eliminate one of the options, and then decide between the two you think may be correct.

1 For each question, choose the correct answer.

08

You will **hear an interview with a boy called Luke, who is going to spend time in the desert.**

1 Luke's father is going to the desert to
  - **A** teach.
  - **B** clean the area.
  - **C** build a medical centre.

2 Luke hopes to
  - **A** record most of the journey with his camera.
  - **B** get more support for the project.
  - **C** reach the camp quickly.

3 Luke may have to
  - **A** limit the time he can use his equipment.
  - **B** borrow some equipment.
  - **C** use his equipment more at the end of the day.

4 What difficulty might Luke have?
  - **A** taking enough clothes
  - **B** staying warm at night
  - **C** keeping cool during the day

5 Luke will eat food that is
  - **A** brought from a different place.
  - **B** provided by the local people.
  - **C** unique to the desert.

6 Luke is anxious because
  - **A** he doesn't know how he'll communicate with people.
  - **B** he might not sleep well.
  - **C** he hasn't travelled to a foreign country before.

Grammar

too and *enough*

1 Complete the second sentence so that it means the same as the first. Use *too* or *enough*.

1 I couldn't eat the soup. It was really hot.
The soup was .... to eat.

2 She's only sixteen years old. She can't get married.
She isn't .... to get married.

3 My house is far from the town centre. I can't walk there.
My house is .... from the town centre to walk there.

4 He's very clever. He can go to a good university.
He's .... to go to a good university.

5 It was very dark. They couldn't see the road.
It was .... to see the road.

6 My jacket isn't warm. I can't wear it for skiing.
My jacket isn't.. to wear it for skiing.

7 My mum's car has got seven seats. She can take all of us to the station.
My mum's car is .... to take all of us to the station.

8 There are a lot of people. We can't give them all free tickets.
There are .... to give them all free tickets.

extremely, fairly, quite, rather, really and *very*

2 Choose the correct option in *italics*.

1 The play was *extremely / fairly* interesting but I thought the second half was a little boring.

2 She worked *really / quite* hard and got top marks for her project.

3 I'm *rather / quite* sure that Ollie's at home now, so let's go and see him.

4 I'm *really / fairly* surprised they went to see that film – they hate sci fi movies.

Prepositions of movement

3 Choose the correct option in *italics*.

1 The detective jumped *into / onto* his car and drove away quickly.

2 She fell as she was getting *off / out of* the taxi and hurt her knee.

3 Have you ever been on a long journey *by / on* ship?

4 Your plane got here *at / on* time, so I didn't have to wait.

5 You should always get *down / off* a horse on the left-hand side.

6 Get *off / out of* the bus at the stop after the museum.

The future

4 Choose the correct option in *italics*.

1 I've just bought a new video game. *I'll bring / I bring* it with me this afternoon.

2 The match *starts / is starting* at 10 am. Don't be late!

3 I can't see you this afternoon. *I'm playing / I'll play* basketball.

4 My sister *will get / is going to get* married next April. Do you want to come to the wedding?

5 When *does the train arrive / is the train arriving*? I can meet you at the station.

6 Thanks for the invitation! *I'll see / I'm going to see* you tomorrow.

5 Complete the dialogues with the verb in brackets. Use *will* or *going to*.

1 **A:** Why are you putting on your coat?
B: I .... (see) a friend.

2 **A:** I'm really thirsty.
B: I .... (get) you some water.

3 **A:** What are your plans for this weekend?
B: I .... (visit) my cousins.

4 **A:** I can't find my wallet.
B: Don't worry. I .... (help) you look for it.

5 **A:** Did you phone Alex?
B: Oh, I forgot. I .... (call) her now.

6 **A:** What do you want to eat, pizza or pasta?
B: I .... (have) pizza, please.

Writing Part 1

- When you finish writing, check verb tenses, spelling and prepositions.

- If you want to change something, cross out the word and write the correct word clearly above it.

Exam advice

1 Look at the exam task and the student's answer below. Correct the <u>underlined</u> mistakes.

Read this email from your English-speaking friend Alex and the notes you have made.

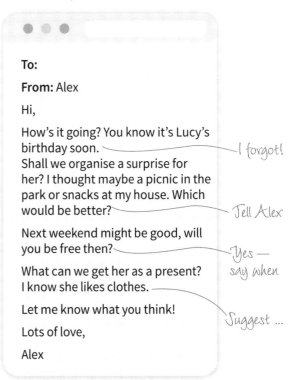

To:

From: Alex

Hi,

How's it going? You know it's Lucy's birthday soon. —— *I forgot!*
Shall we organise a surprise for her? I thought maybe a picnic in the park or snacks at my house. Which would be better? —— *Tell Alex*

Next weekend might be good, will you be free then? —— *Yes — say when*

What can we get her as a present? I know she likes clothes. —— *Suggest ...*

Let me know what you think!

Lots of love,

Alex

Write your email to Alex, using all the notes.

Hi Alex,

I didn't remember Lucy's birthday! We must do something to celebrate. Both your ideas are great, but I'd like to go **(1)** <u>at</u> the park. I expect it'll be **(2)** <u>suny</u> next weekend, so we can eat outside. Next Saturday I'm going to see my grandparents **(3)** <u>to</u> lunch but Sunday is perfect.

Why don't we buy Lucy some **(4)** <u>sunglass</u>? They **(5)** <u>are</u> useful for the picnic and for the rest of the summer. I **(6)** <u>have seen</u> some really nice ones **(7)** <u>on</u> a shop yesterday. Is that a good idea? If you agree, I **(8)** <u>buy</u> them on my way home from school.

Bye for now,

Ryan

2 Write your own answer to the task in Exercise 1 in about 100 words. Remember to check your work.

8 Influencers

Vocabulary

Phrasal verbs

1 Complete the text with the correct form of the phrasal verbs in the box.

> bring up   find out   get on   grow up   make up
> run out of   set up   take up

Why I play chess

When I was a child I used to
(1)........................stories all the time and
I wanted to become a famous writer. Now, I'm
not famous, but I **am** a writer! My parents
were quite strict. They **(2)**........................
my brother and me without any electronics or
TV, so we **(3)**........................with books and
games. We used to start a chess game at the
beginning of the week and we tried to finish
it by the weekend. Sometimes we
(4)........................ time, so we continued
playing on Sunday. My brother and
I generally **(5)**........................well
with each other except when one of us
(6)........................that the other had moved
a chess piece in secret.

I still play now that I'm an adult. Last year
I even **(7)**........................electronic chess,
although playing against the computer isn't
as much fun as playing with my brother.
This year I'm planning to **(8)**........................
a chess club in the village where I live.

Describing people

2 Correct the adjective in bold with an adjective that means the opposite. You are given the first letter.

1 Our football coach is very **easy-going** and makes us train for six hours every week. s ....

2 John is very **hard-working** and spends a lot of time on the sofa watching TV. l ....

3 Tamara's so **stupid**, I'm sure she'll get a good job in the future. c ....

4 The street was **noisy** because there was no traffic. q ....

5 My uncle gave me a new phone for my birthday. He's so **mean**. g ....

6 Don't push in front of other people, Jack! It's **polite**. r ....

7 They felt **calm** as they were waiting for news of the election. a ....

8 She's very **shy** and loves talking in public. c ....

3 Complete the sentences with an adjective formed from the word in brackets.

1 My best friend always seems .... , even when things aren't going well. (cheer)

2 The train service here is .... The trains are always late. (reliable)

3 Human babies are .... for much longer than most animals. (help)

4 She looks .... in that long dress. (beauty)

5 The weather was so .... that we had to cancel the barbecue. (pleasant)

6 He's always telling lies. He's completely .... (honest)

7 The book became a .... film and it won an Oscar. (success)

8 I found your instructions very .... and managed to set up the computer by myself. (help)

9 Marc gets angry quickly if he has to wait. He's so .... (patient)

10 Lizzie won't talk to me. I don't know why she's so .... (friendly)

4 Complete the sentences with words from the box.

> bald beard blonde broad curly dark grey
> long moustache pale short straight wavy

1 She's got

..........................,

..........................,

.... hair.

2 He's got

..........................,

.... , brown

hair and ....

shoulders.

3 She's got long,

.... hair

and ....

skin.

4 He's got long,

..........................,

.... hair

and a ....

5 He's ....

and he's got a black

....

Reading Part 6

1   For each question, write the correct answer. Write one word in each gap.

Influences

When we decide to buy a particular product or take up a particular activity, we usually think we are making an independent decision. Often, we don't realise **(1)** .... much we are influenced by the people around us and the messages we receive.

One influence is clearly our family. **(2)** .... your parents are interested in travelling, for example, then probably you will be, too. Or sometimes we like to show we are different from others, so we choose a sport or a hobby that no one in our family **(3)** .... done before.

Friends' attitudes and opinions affect us, too. We often want to be like **(4)** .... so sometimes we copy what they do. Advertising also influences us more **(5)** .... we think. Frequent messages about a particular food or drink, with images of young people having fun, make us think that we should **(6)** .... least try it.

Grammar
Zero, first and second conditionals

1 Complete the sentences with the correct form of the verb in brackets
to make zero, first and second conditionals. Write 0, 1 or 2 next to the sentence.

1 Jemma will be pleased if she .... (get) that job. ....
2 I .... (tell) my parents if I had a problem. ....
3 Next week I'll be in Paris if my plans .... (go) well. ....
4 .... (you / travel) by plane if you had enough money? ....
5 If you ask my cousin, he .... (give) you some good advice. ....
6 If Tom .... (wake up) late, he doesn't usually have breakfast. ....
7 If they were smarter, they .... (not do) such stupid things. ....
8 If I .... (find) a good video on the internet, I send the link to my friends. ....

when, *if* and *unless*

2 Complete the sentences with *when, if* or *unless*.

1 I've lost my phone. .... anyone finds it, please put it on my desk.
2 I wouldn't have a dog as a pet .... I had a garden.
3 I'd sleep all morning on Saturday .... I didn't have an interview at 9 o'clock.
4 Lucas always checks his blog .... he gets up in the morning.
5 She'll be worried about you .... you phone her to say where you are.
6 We set up the YouTube channel .... we started selling our products.
7 I'd like to be a volunteer .... I leave school.
8 You won't become famous .... a lot of people see your videos.

3 Match the beginnings and endings of the sentences and complete them
with *if, when* or *unless*.

1 I'll wait for you in the café
2 I don't usually lend money to friends
3 It's hard to speak in front of a lot of people
4 We only follow famous people online
5 He'll need to check in
6 I won't buy those trousers
7 You shouldn't put their photos on your blog
8 We'll be happy to see you

a .... they give their permission.
b .... he gets to the airport.
c .... they give interesting advice.
d .... you're very confident.
e .... you come to London next week.
f .... it's an emergency.
g .... your train is late.
h .... the price is reduced.

Listening Part 3

Exam advice

- Is the missing information a number, a date, a time, a person, etc.? Try to decide what words you might hear before you listen.
- Write numbers in figures (e.g. 4 or 10) not in words (e.g. four or ten) so you don't make spelling mistakes with numbers.

1 For each question, write the correct answer in the gap. Write one or two words or a number or a date or a time.

09

You will hear a boy giving a class presentation about a teenage girl called Mikaila, who helps to protect bees.

Mikaila Ulmer

Mikaila's (1) .... taught her not to be afraid of bees.

The ingredients of her great-grandmother's recipe include (2) .... and honey.

The Ulmer family set up a company after (3) .... bought Mikaila's lemonade.

Mikaila gives advice to (4) .... who want to set up a business.

The most important things in her life are her family and (5) ....

If bees disappear, (6) .... will be affected.

Writing Part 2 (An article)

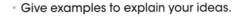

Exam advice

- Write your answer in two or three paragraphs. Each paragraph should answer one or two of the questions.
- Give examples to explain your ideas.

1 Read this exam task and the student's article below. Find five spelling mistakes and five punctuation mistakes.

You see this notice in an international English-language magazine for teenagers.

Articles wanted!

WHAT MAKES A GOOD FRIEND?

What kind of character should a good friend have?

Should a good friend have the same hobbies and opinions as you? Why?

Write an article answering these questions and we will publish the best ones.

Write your article.

Having a good friend is the best thing in the world. Good friends litsen to your problems and are generos friendly and easy-going.

Freinds laugh together and often enjoy doing the same things but its not so important if your friend likes footbal and you like a different sport You can still be friends.

My best friend is Hassan. I only see him at school because he lives in another town, but we have funn in the breaks. He's good at maths and I'm good at english, so we help each other in class. When we leave school I'm sure we'll continue to be friends.

---

2 Write your own answer to the task in Exercise 1 in about 100 words. Check your spelling and punctuation.

9 Stay fit and healthy

Listening Part 2

Exam advice

- Don't worry if you don't understand everything. It's not necessary to understand every word you hear. You only need to understand the parts of the recording that answer the questions.

- The words you hear will not always be the same as in the question. Think about different words that can mean the same.

1 For each question, choose the correct answer.

1 You will hear a boy telling his friend about basketball training.
Why did he miss the training last week?
- **A** He had flu.
- **B** He was worried about a test.
- **C** His mum couldn't take him.

2 You will hear two friends talking about a table tennis competition.
What does the boy say about it?
- **A** It's an opportunity to meet new people.
- **B** It's a change from their routine.
- **C** It's important that they win.

3 You will hear a girl telling her friend about a football match she went to.
She was disappointed because
- **A** someone's behaviour bothered her.
- **B** the weather was terrible.
- **C** her team played badly.

4 You will hear two friends talking about a trip to a science museum.
What do they agree about?
- **A** how much they learnt from it
- **B** how interesting the staff were
- **C** how well objects were displayed

5 You will hear a boy talking to his mother.
Why was the boy unable to call her?
- **A** He didn't have time to do it.
- **B** His phone didn't work.
- **C** He didn't have his phone with him.

6 You will hear two friends talking about going skiing.
The girl tells the boy
- **A** to be careful of other skiers.
- **B** to buy good equipment.
- **C** to expect to fall.

Vocabulary

Sports

1 Choose the correct option in *italics* and write the name of the sport. Use the photos to help you.

1 The Wolves *beat / won* the Tigers two goals to one in the match yesterday.

....

2 Both athletes got the gold medal because they *drew / scored* in the final.

....

3 He used a *bat / helmet* to hit the ball.

....

4 You wear thick *trainers / gloves* and heavy boots.

....

5 He broke his *bat / racket* when he fell on the wet court.

....

6 The *track / score* was 24–25 to the other team when I hit the ball into the net, so we lost.

....

2 Complete the text with the words in the box.

| bike   breath   exercise   exhausted   mountain biking |
| rollerblading   skateboard   surfers |

WHEELS AND FITNESS

The invention of the wheel didn't only improve transport, but also produced many sporting activities. The two wheels on a **(1)** .... can take you much faster and further than your two feet. The inventor of **(2)** .... decided to put a line of wheels on his shoes.

Some people say the **(3)** .... was invented by **(4)** .... who wanted the same experience on land as on the sea, so they put wheels on small boards. Although wheels can help us move more easily, these forms of **(5)** .... still require a lot of energy. **(6)** .... up and down tracks in the countryside certainly keeps you fit, and skateboarding will leave you out of **(7)** .... as much as jogging. I tried rollerblading for the first time the other day, and after an hour, I was **(8)** ....!

Illnesses and accidents

3 Match the beginnings and endings of these sentences.

1 If you have earache,
2 When you have flu,
3 If you sprain your ankle,
4 When you cut yourself,
5 Doctors will take an X-ray
6 When you injure yourself,
7 Doctors sometimes recommend a blood test
8 You should keep your neck warm

a sometimes you get a bruise.
b take a pill, like an aspirin.
c you'll need to put a bandage on it.
d you usually have a high temperature.
e if you have a fever.
f if you have a cough.
g put a plaster on.
h if they think you have fractured a bone.

Reading Part 3

Exam advice

- Read the whole text first before you look at the questions.
- For each question, find the words in the text that tell you which option to choose.

1 For each question, choose the correct answer.

Katie Swan

Many young tennis stars were given a racket almost as soon as they could walk and played seriously from an early age. But this was not the case for Katie Swan. She had her first tennis lesson when she was seven, just for fun, when she was on holiday in Portugal with her family and they wanted her to have something to do while they were there. Her parents laughed when the coach said she would be a professional one day, but his words came true.

Katie Swan was born in Bristol in 1999, and is one of the most promising young tennis players from the UK. After her Portuguese holiday she signed up for tennis classes and began to spend more time on the court, but she didn't give up other activities for the sport. She played competitive hockey and did well at school. After a few years, she and her family moved to the USA and she went to a local school there, not because of the tennis opportunities, but because her father's job took her

family there. She could also enjoy more hours of sunshine to play outdoors and her game quickly improved.

When she was 15, she was proud to reach number two in the world as a junior player, and then, the following year, she played very well for the British team. Doing a lot of sport and training so much can be hard on a player's body and Katie has suffered from back pain. When she was 17, she was upset because an injury to her foot meant that she couldn't finish the Wimbledon tournament in London that year.

Now that Katie's older, she says the lifestyle of a professional tennis player is a challenge. It's not always easy being away from home and spending all your time in strange hotels. She loves competing though, especially when she wins, which she does quite often. Katie has certainly become more confident by playing in international competitions, but she still feels nervous before an important match.

1 When Katie was seven
- **A** a teacher recognised her talent.
- **B** her parents wanted her to become a professional tennis player.
- **C** her family gave her a tennis racket.
- **D** she persuaded her parents to let her play tennis.

2 She went to live in the USA because
- **A** she wanted to concentrate more on her tennis.
- **B** the weather was better for sporting activities.
- **C** she needed to go to a better school.
- **D** her father had to work there.

3 What disappointment did she have in her late teens?
- **A** She didn't become number one among the junior players.
- **B** She didn't have time to train enough.
- **C** She couldn't win an important competition.
- **D** She didn't play in international competitions.

4 What does she enjoy most about being a professional tennis player?
- **A** the experience of travelling to lots of different places
- **B** the pleasure of competition
- **C** the feeling she has when she is about to play
- **D** playing international matches

5 What would be a good title for this article?
- **A** A star whose family gave up everything for her career
- **B** A great future for a player who never loses
- **C** A childhood ambition becomes a reality
- **D** The good times and the bad times of a sports professional

Grammar

Relative clauses

1 Complete the sentences with the correct relative pronoun – *which, that, who, whose, when* or *where*.

1 This is the athlete .... won the 100m race.
2 The runner, ... trainers were old, couldn't run very well.
3 Matt, ... was taking part in the bike race, was injured when he hit a rock.
4 The best time to go surfing is in the morning, ... the waves are bigger.
5 It's the most famous court in the UK, ... the Wimbledon tennis final is played.
6 The sports centre, ... was built in 1950, now needs to be repaired.
7 Did you see the golf player .... ball went into the lake?
8 I'd really like to buy some trainers .... are specially made for running.

2 Make one sentence from 1–6 using a relative pronoun and making any other necessary changes.

1 There's the man. He lives in the flat next door.

There's the man ....

....

2 That's the girl. Her mother was my nurse in hospital.

That's the girl ....

....

3 2010 was the year. Our team won the cup.

2010 was the year ....

....

4 This is the church. My parents got married here.

This is the church ....

....

5 My only brother moved to Australia. He is a pilot.

My only brother, ...

.... ,

moved to Australia.

6 The cinema opened last week. It had been closed for years.

The cinema, ...

.... ,

opened last week.

Past perfect

3 Complete the sentences with the verb in brackets in the past simple or past perfect.

1 Her grandad was feeling weak because he .... (have) an operation.
2 When we .... (play) the match we all went out for a meal.
3 Why .... (you / go) home before the match had ended?
4 I went to see the nurse because I .... (hurt) my leg.
5 .... (Ryan / give up) football by the time he was thirty?
6 When I got home I realised I .... (not pick up) my keys that morning.
7 Eva .... (not finish) talking when Alex interrupted her.

Writing Part 2 (A story)

> **Exam advice**
> - You can connect sentences in the story with words like *then, next, finally*, etc.
> - You can make the story interesting by using words like *suddenly, luckily*, etc.

1 Look at the exam task and complete the student's answer with the words from the box.

Your English teacher has asked you to write a story.
Your story must begin with this sentence.
It was the most important day of my life.

after finally luckily suddenly then when

It was the most important day of my life. That day I got up early and I was ready to go (1) .... my friend knocked on the door. I said goodbye to my brother and (2) .... we went to the sports centre, where we saw lots of people waiting to go in to see the regional gymnastics competition. (3) .... , our coach had given us special passes to go in the side door because we were going to compete.
When we got inside, we found the rest of the team. Everyone looked fantastic. (4) .... , we heard our names and it was our turn to perform. (5) .... the performance we waited anxiously. (6) .... , they called our names again. We had won!

2 Now answer this exam task.

Your English teacher has asked you to write a story.
Your story must begin with this sentence.
Sam was both anxious and excited when leaving the house.

Write your story in about 100 words.

10 Looks amazing!

> **Exam advice**
>
> - Read the description of the first person, then quickly scan the texts to find one that matches what they want.
> - Do the same with all five people. Then read the texts you have chosen more carefully to check they are exactly right.

1 The people below all want to go shopping. Read the descriptions of eight shopping areas. Decide which shopping area would be the most suitable for each person.

1 Jamila's going to a party tonight and wants to buy something new to wear, but she hasn't got much money. She also has to get a cake for the party.

2 Chen's going to stay with a family abroad and wants to buy a present for the teenage son, who is into music. He wants something original and he hasn't got much space in his suitcase.

3 Karan's working till 8 pm but he wants to buy a present, like a bracelet or a necklace, for a friend's birthday tomorrow. He wants something she can take back if she doesn't like it.

4 Niran needs some new football boots. He's not sure what kind to buy, so he wants to try a variety of styles and wants someone to help him choose.

5 Melanie wants to buy a good-quality garden chair that she'll be able to leave outside all year round. She'll have to take her car to bring it home.

Where to shop guide:

A Centre Place

This shopping centre has a number of shops specialising in outdoor activities. Don't miss the footwear stores, where you can get expert advice on a wide range of makes and models. You can also find camping goods, such as lightweight chairs and tables, and fishing equipment. Late-night closing on Fridays and Saturdays.

B SMITH'S

All you could want for sports fans. 20,000 m² of clothes and equipment for athletes, hikers, team sports players, etc. Modern shopping means you simply choose what you want and pay at the automatic checkout. With no queuing, you'll be in and out in a moment. Open till 10 pm every day. Free parking for customers.

C Holly Corner

This area of small expensive boutiques is a must for shoppers who love stylish clothes and classic gifts. The jewellery shops will offer you a personal service to help you decide on just the right item. Visit the Vintage Café for tea and a slice of delicious homemade cake after the shops close at 5 pm.

D Newton Cross

A five-floor department store, famous for their wide range of gold and silver jewellery and good-quality clothes. Shopping here is easy because goods can be returned with no questions asked, although it can be more expensive than other shops in the area. Open 10 am – 10 pm every day. Car park on the lower levels.

Oak Lane

E

This street market, held every day in the pedestrian zone, offers a variety of stalls selling small kitchen items and garden products, fresh food, and much more. You can find fashionable dresses, trousers and T-shirts printed with the faces of famous singers or sports stars at low prices. Don't miss the tasty products from Sam's Bakery. Open 8.00 to 15.00.

HIGHVIEW CENTRE

F

Highview Centre is located outside the city but has a large parking area for customers. This shopping centre offers all you could want for the home. They have a wide range of furniture suitable for both outdoor and indoor use, from cheap and cheerful plastic to stronger and more solid varieties that will last for years. Open every day except Sundays, 9.00–21.00.

north end

G

An unusual mix of stalls in this market sell goods for music lovers, such as second-hand guitars and violins, locally grown plants and flowers, and organic foods such as cheese, meat and homemade jams. Parking can be difficult, so go early. Open from 8.00 to 15.00.

Satton Street

H

A US-style shopping mall with fast-food restaurants, cheap doughnut cafés and electronics shops which will attract young people. You can find the latest in technology such as mini-headphones or fitness watches. Every week there are new devices that you've never seen before. Open till 8 pm.

Vocabulary

course, dish, food, meal and *plate*

1 Complete the sentences with the correct option in *italics*.

1 Some people say the most important *food / meal* of the day is breakfast.
2 What time of day do they have their *main / large* meal in China?
3 In my country we usually have three *plates / courses* at lunchtime.
4 The speciality in that restaurant is a spicy chicken *dish / meal*.
5 The best *meal / food* in town is served in the Turkish restaurant.
6 What would you like for *starters / dessert*? Ice cream, chocolate mousse or fruit?
7 I have an allergy to dairy *produces / products* so I don't drink cow's milk.
8 I'm playing in a match this afternoon, so I only want a *short / light* lunch.

Shops and services

2 Complete the sentences.

1 They went to the .... to borrow a book.
2 He took his car to the .... in the next town to have it repaired.
3 We went to the .... to get a loaf of bread.
4 Can you go to the .... to get some aspirin for me?
5 She bought the novel in the local ....
6 I had my hair dyed at the .... last week.
7 My tooth is hurting, so I need to go to the ....
8 You can't wash that leather jacket. You'll have to take it to the ....

3 Complete the sentences with a word from the box.

> book   borrow   buy   complain   make

1 There's no need to buy a map. We can .... one from the library.
2 Will you phone the hotel to .... a room for tomorrow night?
3 If you want to see the doctor, you'll have to .... an appointment.
4 He lost his phone charger, so he had to .... another one.
5 The coach on my diving course was terrible. I'm going to .... to the sports centre.

Grammar
have something done

1 Complete sentence B so that it means the same as sentence A. Use *have something done*.

1 A Someone cleans my car every Saturday.
  B I ....
  every Saturday.

2 A Did someone paint their kitchen?
  B Did they .... ?

3 A Someone brings her shopping to the house.
  B She ....
  to the house.

4 A A famous chef is making their wedding cake.
  B They ....
  by a famous chef.

5 A Someone takes a photo of their family once a year.
  B They ....
  once a year.

6 A Does someone prepare her meals?
  B Does she .... ?

Commands and instructions

2 Complete the instructions with the correct form of the verbs in the box.

> accept   buy   not forget   not invite   make
> send   think   use

How to plan the best party:

1 First, ... about the number of people.

2 .... too many people.

3 If friends offer to help, ... their offers.

4 .... the invitations a couple of weeks before the date.

5 .... the fresh food on the day of the party.

6 .... simple dishes that don't take long to prepare.

7 .... paper plates and cups so you don't have to wash up.

8 Finally, ... the neighbours may not like loud music!

Listening Part 1

1 For each question, choose the correct answer.

11 1 What was the man unhappy with at the restaurant?

  A   **B**   **C**

2 Where is the girl going?

  A   **B**   **C**

3 What did the boy forget?

  A   **B**   **C**

4 What does the boy want to borrow?

  A   **B**   **C**

5 How much will the woman pay for the meal?

A   B   C

6 Where will the boy go first after school?

A   B   C

7 Which film does the reviewer recommend?

A   B   C

Now match the questions (1–5) to the student's notes below.

1 What can you do to feel healthier in general?
2 Should you eat well?
3 Should you sleep well?
4 Should you do exercise?
5 Why is it important to have a healthy lifestyle?

a
FRESH FOOD

b
ENJOY LIFE

c
COMBINATION OF ALL THREE THINGS – DIET, SLEEP, EXERCISE

d
SPORT – TWICE A WEEK

e
8 OR 9 HOURS

f
EAT LOTS OF FRUIT AND VEGETABLES

g
WALK NOT CAR

h
FEEL HAPPY

i
DON'T MISS IMPORTANT MEALS

2 Read Patrick's article. Did he answer all the questions?

In my opinion, a healthy lifestyle is a combination of food, sleep and exercise. If you eat well but you don't do any exercise, you can't be healthy.

It's essential to eat fresh food. For example, in my family we buy meat from the butcher's and we don't eat too much fast food. We also have fruit and vegetables with every meal. I think breakfast is an important meal if you want to have energy for the day.

You should also try to do exercise. Maybe do a sport twice a week or walk instead of going by car. If you are healthy, you will feel happy and enjoy life.

3 Write your own answer to the task in Exercise 1 in about 100 words. Make notes, organise your answer in paragraphs and answer all the questions.

Writing Part 2 (An article)

- Think about who will be reading your article.
- Try to use varied vocabulary and not to repeat the same words.

Exam advice

1 Read this exam task.

You see this notice in an English-language magazine for teenagers.

Articles wanted!

A HEALTHY LIFESTYLE
What kind of things can you do to feel healthier?
Eat well, sleep well, do exercise – or all of these things?
Is it important to you to be healthy? Why? / Why not?
The best articles will be published next month.

Write your article.

Looks amazing!

11 The natural world

Listening Part 4

Exam advice

- You won't hear the exact same words in the recording that appear in the questions and options.
- You have time before the listening starts to read the questions and options.

1 For each question, choose the correct answer.

12

You will hear an interview with a teenager from Bermuda called Magnus, who helps to protect the oceans and the wildlife in them.

1 Magnus first became interested in the problem of pollution in the sea when
  A he found some examples of it.
  B he was given a book about it.
  C he attended a talk about it.

2 The first thing he did after becoming a member of an environmental group was
  A to count the number of different plants.
  B to test new equipment.
  C to help scientists to get information.

3 Magnus learnt that people
  A don't realise the danger of some products.
  B don't get ill from eating contaminated food.
  C don't care about what they throw away.

4 What advice does Magnus give to people who want to help to protect sea life?
  A start an environmental organisation
  B avoid items with certain ingredients
  C stop eating fish

5 What does Magnus think has been his greatest achievement so far?
  A showing visitors to his island what the problem is
  B improving the beaches in his area
  C encouraging more people to visit the aquarium

6 What does Magnus want to do next?
  A study environmental science
  B work for an environmental charity
  C take part in environmental projects on his island

Grammar
The passive

1 Rewrite the sentences to make them passive.

1 Someone stole my wallet from my bag.
  My wallet .... from my bag.
2 People don't use public phones any more.
  Public phones .... any more.
3 A loud noise woke them up.
  They .... by a loud noise.
4 Lions often hunt zebras.
  Zebras .... by lions.
5 Lots of people watched the wildlife documentary.
  The wildlife documentary ....
  by lots of people.
6 They created the national park in 1995.
  The national park .... in 1995.
7 The wind didn't blow the tree down.
  The tree .... by the wind.
8 They protect the animals from hunters.
  The animals .... from hunters.

2 Put the words in order to make questions.

1 organisation / was / set / When / up / the / environmental?

....

....

2 taken / for / the / Where / recycling / rubbish / is?

....

....

3 given / results / the / the / were / to / When / students?

....

....

4 animals / captured / are / How /the?

....

....

5 you / countryside / in / brought / Were / up / the?

....

....

6 animals / Are / the / well / looked / zoo / the / after / in?

....

....

3 Complete the letter to a newspaper with the present or past simple passive form of the verbs in brackets.

Letters

Dear Editor,

We are students from Year 11 in Hollyhill School and we are writing to you to express our concern about the government's decision not to make the Black Mountain area into a National Park.

The area **(1)** .... (use) by many people for picnics at weekends and in summer. But if this area **(2)** .... (not / protect), then the animals will disappear. Last year many trees **(3)** .... (cut down) to make a road, and a fence **(4)** .... (built) along the road so animals can't cross it.

A project **(5)** .... (set up) by our school to help protect the wildlife in our mountains and last year many kilos of rubbish **(6)** .... (pick up) by volunteers, but if people **(7)** .... (not / prevent) from entering the area, then the problem will continue.

If this letter **(8)** .... (read) by lots of people who feel the same as us, maybe we can work together to solve the problem.

Yours sincerely,

Class 11B

Comparative and superlative adverbs

4 Complete the sentences with an adverb from the box in the comparative or superlative form.

> badly carefully easily fast hard quietly
> slowly well

1 The ostrich runs .... of any bird but it can't fly!

2 I let my sister ask for the train tickets when we were in London because she speaks English much .... than I do.

3 You must move .... through the jungle or you will frighten the animals away with the noise!

4 Next time you should check your work .... You made some basic mistakes.

5 The tiny rabbit ran .... than the others and was the last to get to the hole.

6 Jasmin found the way to the meeting point .... than she expected, so she arrived very early.

7 The player who trained .... was asked to play in the first team.

8 My brother behaved .... of all the students on the trip, so he wasn't allowed to go on the next one.

Vocabulary
Animals

1 Find the words for eight animals. Then complete the sentences below.

B	E	A	D	C	I	N	G	K
R	P	E	N	G	U	I	N	A
T	K	C	H	E	O	D	I	N
I	F	A	N	O	S	R	U	G
G	U	M	B	Y	T	C	M	A
E	P	E	E	L	R	A	T	R
R	F	L	A	M	I	N	G	O
L	G	A	R	T	C	I	S	O
B	E	L	E	P	H	A	N	T

1 An .... has a trunk and big ears.
2 A .... can go a long time without drinking.
3 A .... is pink and often stands on one leg.
4 A .... is a member of the cat family.
5 An .... has a long neck and wings.
6 A .... lays eggs and can swim.
7 A .... likes eating honey.
8 A .... stands on two legs and jumps.

Noun suffixes

2 Complete the sentences with a noun made from the word in brackets.

1 Have you received .... of your flight from the airline yet? (confirm)
2 We had a .... about the problem of global warming. (discuss)
3 They sent us an .... to the conference. (invite)
4 .... is a serious problem in many major cities. (pollute)
5 The screen I ordered online was broken, so I asked for a .... (replace)
6 This app will give you the .... of a word in 50 different languages. (translate)
7 The .... of the audience grew when they heard that the first prize was an African safari. (excite)
8 The .... of technology has helped us to protect animals in danger of extinction. (develop)

3 Correct the mistakes with nouns in these sentences.

1 The scientists made an ~~announceation~~ that they had found a new species. ......*announcement*......
2 All children have the right to a good educateion. ....
3 After the completement of the project, he wrote a report. ....
4 One of the most important invents in history was the wheel. ....
5 Amy's disappointing was clear when she missed the trip to the zoo. ....
6 The only entertaination in the town is the local cinema. ....

Reading Part 5

1 For each question, choose the correct answer.

Rhinos

Rhinos are some of the largest animals in the world. They liv[e] Africa and Asia in tropical rai[n] **(1)** .... and grasslands. The biggest **(2)** .... can wei[gh] 2,400 kilos, which is the weig[ht] of thirty men. Although they [are] very big and strong, they don'[t] **(3)** .... other animals, but instead they feed on lots of grass and other plants. In fact, they spend all day and nig[ht] eating. What rhinos really love is being in or near water, where they can **(4)** .... cool. They generally live on the[ir] own, except for the **(5)** .... relationship they have with oxpeckers. These are small birds that sit on rhinos and he[lp] keep them free of insects. Rhinos only have one **(6)** .... – humans, who kill them to take their horn. Since the beginning of the 20th century their population has fallen from 500,000 to only 29,000 now living in the wild.

	A		B		C		D	
1	A	trees	B	woods	C	coasts	D	forests
2	A	species	B	wildlife	C	range	D	set
3	A	chase	B	catch	C	hunt	D	benefit
4	A	keep	B	take	C	have	D	make
5	A	separate	B	unusual	C	complete	D	real
6	A	danger	B	competitor	C	enemy	D	injury

Writing Part 1

Look at the exam task and answer the questions.

1 What did you tell Freddie in your last email?
2 Which four things must you put in your reply?

Read this email from your friend Freddie and the notes you have made.

To:

From: Freddie

Hi,

I'm happy to hear you have finished your exams. If you aren't busy, would you like to stay at my place next weekend? — *Yes!*

While you're here, the environmental club I belong to needs some volunteers. We could either help pick up litter along the river or plant trees in a park for a few hours. Which activity would you prefer? — *Say which*

We have to wear old clothes and boots for these kinds of activities. I have an extra pair of boots if you want to borrow them. — *No, because...*

What else do you want to do during your stay? — *Tell Freddie*

All the best,

Freddie

Write your email to Freddie, using all the notes.

---

2 Read the answer from Ryan and choose the correct option in *italics*.

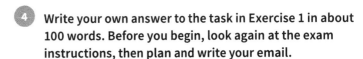

Hi Freddie,

(1) *I love / I'd love* to get together next weekend, especially as I now **(2)** *have / am having* more free time.

The environmental club sounds fun! I'd rather help to plant trees, I think. I **(3)** *did / have done* that last year in the park near my house and the trees **(4)** *already grew / have already grown* taller. I **(5)** *love / loved* nature, so I like to protect the environment.

Can we visit the national park near your village, too? I remember it was so beautiful last spring. We could take a picnic if the weather **(6)** *is / will be* nice.

Anyway, **(7)** *I'll be / I am* at your house early on Saturday morning.

I can't wait to see you,

Cheers,

Ryan

3 Read the answer again. Did Ryan include all four points in the reply?

4 Write your own answer to the task in Exercise 1 in about 100 words. Before you begin, look again at the exam instructions, then plan and write your email.

12 Express yourself!

Listening Part 3

> **Exam advice**
> - If you miss one of the words, just move on to the next question. You will hear the recording a second time.
> - Check your answers carefully in the second listening.

1 For each question, write the correct answer in the gap. Write one or two words or a number or a date or a time.

You will hear a teenager called Jemma talking about a video-making course she went on last year.

Jemma's video-making course

Jemma's visit to a (1) .... started her interest in film-making.

She attended the course on Saturday mornings except in the month of (2) .... when she also went in the afternoon.

Examples of the videos they made are: giving advice about (3) ...., dance classes or performances of plays.

The groups had to take their own (4) .... to use in the videos.

She especially enjoyed the (5) .... at the end of the course.

She wants to learn more about (6) ....

Vocabulary

Collocations: using your phone

1 Complete the sentences with a verb.

1 I always use my phone to .... the time. I don't have a watch.

2 I don't often .... friends. I prefer to send them a text message.

3 I like to .... games on my phone. I especially like *Clash Royale*.

4 I love to .... selfies when I go on a trip. I want to see myself with a memorable background.

5 I don't often .... online when I don't have wifi. It uses too much data.

6 I use Instagram to .... videos with my friends. We watch them and pass them on if they are funny.

7 I usually .... friends when I want to see them. I rarely phone them because a quick message is much easier.

8 I often .... music on my phone when I'm travelling on public transport – with headphones, of course!

ask, ask for, speak, talk, say and *tell*

2 Choose the correct option in *italics*.

1 Would you ever *say / tell / speak* a lie if it could help someone?

2 Sarah can *talk / tell / speak* Italian perfectly because she lived in Italy for 10 years.

3 Mark was tired when he got home, so he *asked / said / told* goodnight to everyone and went straight to bed.

4 Now I have social media, I don't *talk / ask / say* to my friends very often on the phone.

5 I was lost, so I went into a shop to *ask for / ask the / ask* help.

6 I wanted to *tell / say / talk* I was sorry, but Jordan didn't listen to me.

7 Can you *speak / ask / tell* me your surname?

8 My coach wants to *talk / say / ask* to my parents about my plans for next year.

Negative prefixes

3 Complete the sentences with the adjectives in the box and a negative prefix – *im-*, *in-* or *un-*.

> believable   comfortable   complete   correct
> expensive   friendly   patient   polite   possible

1 It's .... to take the last biscuit on the plate.
2 We lost one of the pieces, so the puzzle is ....
3 You have to wait. Don't be so ....!
4 It was an .... concert with amazing sound and a great audience!
5 If your answer is ...., then the other team gets a turn.
6 This problem is .... to solve. We'll never work it out.
7 The bed in the hotel was really ...., so I didn't sleep well.
8 Dancing is a fun and .... way to keep fit.
9 No one spoke to me at the party. They were really ....

Reading Part 4

- Look at linking words and expressions like *before that, afterwards, later, in addition,* to help you decide which sentence is missing.
- Look at pronouns (e.g. *they / their / them; we / our / us*) in the sentences before and after the spaces to see if they make logical and grammatical sense.

Exam advice

1 Five sentences have been removed from the text. For each question, choose the correct answer. There are three extra sentences which you do not need to use.

A No one really knows the things they are saying.
B Later we went to see the dolphins in the ocean.
C My team chose to find out how dolphins communicate.
D They enjoyed swimming in the sea with the dolphins.
E We want to make people realise the importance of keeping the sea clean.
F Because they couldn't see, they had to do this using their voices.
G That's how scientists know they're marine animals, not fish.
H Dolphins find out what's around them by using clicking noises.

LEARNING ABOUT DOLPHINS

My experience volunteering at a dolphin centre over the summer

I live in Western Australia, where there are loads of marine animals, but dolphins are among my favourites, so when I saw an advert for teenagers to take part in a volunteer project called *Dolphin Days*, I decided to join. As volunteers we had to work in groups to create information sessions and activities for children visiting the centre. This meant doing our own research about dolphins and deciding what was most interesting. **(1)** .... We discovered that scientists think they actually have conversations with each other! **(2)** ....The dolphins may be talking about where the best fish are or if there is a dangerous shark in the area.

We can hear some of the noises dolphins make but they also make other sounds, which the human ear can't hear. I was surprised to find out that they find food using 'echolocation'. This is when a sound travels to an object, which gives an 'echo' – the sound comes back and can be heard again. **(3)** ....When they hear their echo, the dolphins know the object's shape and size, and can decide if it is a fish or octopus, which might be good to eat, or just a rock.

The volunteer group I took part in invented an activity that was a lot of fun. First, we covered the children's eyes with a scarf. Then, they had to try and find different objects in the room. **(4)** ....They discovered that if you go closer to an object, like a box, you can hear the sound coming back from it, but you have to listen very carefully!

These Dolphin Days were only a small part of a project to teach people that our oceans need to be respected and protected. **(5)** .... This is essential to provide a safe home for the wildlife there.

Grammar
Reported speech

1 Rewrite the sentences in reported speech.

1 Jeff said, 'I don't want to go out late.'

Jeff said .... to go out late.

2 Martha said, 'We are leaving in the morning.'

Martha said .... in the morning.

3 He said, 'Zoe will come over at ten o'clock.'

He said .... at ten o'clock.

4 She said, 'Harry's lived in that house all his life.'

She said .... in that house all his life.

5 Sue said, 'I enjoyed the trip very much.'

Sue said .... the trip very much.

6 The teacher said to us, 'You can't leave the room before the end of the test.'

The teacher said .... the room before the end of the test.

Reported questions

2 Correct the mistakes in the direct questions.

1 John asked me if I was going to China.

John asked me, '~~Were you going~~ to China?'

Are you going

2 Gwen asked her teacher when he would give them the results.

Gwen asked her teacher, 'When would you give us the results?'

....

3 Kevin asked Linda how many people Mia had invited to the party.

Kevin asked Linda, 'How many people have you invited to the party?'

....

4 Anne asked Jack if he wanted to go to the beach.

Anne asked Jack, 'Do you wanted to go to the beach?'

....

5 Robin asked me why I couldn't stay longer.

Robin asked me, 'Why can't I stay longer?'

....

6 Jo asked Jenny where she had bought that dress.

Jo asked Jenny, 'Where do you buy that dress?'

....

Reported commands

3 Look at the instructions for taking an exam and complete the reported commands.

1 'Write clearly.'

The teacher told us ....

2 'Don't use a pen.'

The teacher told us ....

3 'Be careful with spelling.'

The teacher told us ....

4 'Don't worry about understanding every word.'

The teacher told us ....

....

5 'Guess the meaning.'

The teacher told us ....

6 'Don't forget to bring an identification document.'

The teacher told us ....

4 Exam candidates often make mistakes with reported speech. Underline the mistakes in the sentences and correct them.

1 My teacher said me that my work was very good.

2 I asked the shop assistant if she can help me.

3 He told to me he would like to come and visit my country.

4 They told me if I wanted to come to their house for dinner.

5 She promised don't tell anybody.

6 I called my friend and told him I found his camera.

Indirect questions

5 Complete the indirect questions.

1 What time is it?
Could you tell me .... ?

2 Can I take a photo?
I was wondering if ....

3 Where is the IT department?
I'd like to know ....

4 How often do you look at your phone?
Could I ask you .... ?

5 Where does Thomas live?
Do you know .... ?

Writing Part 2 (A story)

> **Exam advice**
>
> • The story should have a beginning, middle and end. Use paragraphs to make this clear.
>
> • You can write what people say as well as what they do in the story. You can use direct or reported speech.

1 Look at this exam task and a student's answer. Number the paragraphs in the correct order.

> Your English teacher has asked you to write a story.
> Your story must begin with this sentence.
> *I was excited when I read the text message!*

A ☐

I shouted, 'Mum! I'm going to Paris to play in the championship!' but she didn't answer. I ran downstairs to find her. Unfortunately, I didn't see that my dog was coming out of the living room.

B ☐

I fell hard on the floor and heard a horrible noise. Then, my arm started to hurt. Mum came out of the kitchen, looked at it and said, 'I think you've broken it!' That was the end of my trip to Paris.

C ☐

I was excited when I read the text message! It was unbelievable! The volleyball club had chosen me to play in the team for the European championship.

2 Write the sentences with the correct punctuation.
Example:
Katie asked where are you going
Katie asked, 'Where are you going?'

1 Lucas said I've hurt my leg

....

....

2 The police officer asked when did you arrive home

....

....

3 Marina announced I'm going to America

....

....

4 Charlie replied I don't know

....

....

3 Write the sentences in Exercise 2 in reported speech.
Example:
Katie asked where I was going.

1

....

2 ....

....

3 ....

....

4 ....

....

4 Now answer this exam task. Write three or four paragraphs: the beginning, the middle and the end.

> Your English teacher has asked you to write a story.
> Your story must begin with this sentence.
> *I slowly opened the box and looked inside.*

Write your story in about 100 words. Try to use direct or reported speech.

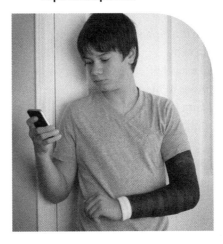

My life and home

1 Complete the crossword.

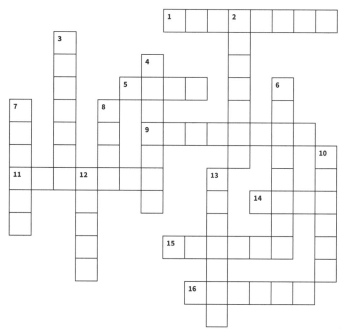

Across

1 My mum always sits in her favourite .... when she wants to watch TV. (8)

5 We went through the front door into the .... (4)

9 Danny, can you put the games in the .... in the living room, please? (8)

11 On weekdays we eat in the ...., not in the dining room. (7)

14 The children sat together on the .... to play the video game. (4)

15 There is space in our .... for two cars. (6)

16 The .... is in the bathroom. We don't have a separate one. (6)

Down

2 The chair in my room is a bit hard so I use a .... to sit on. (7)

3 It's cold so I'll put an extra .... on your bed. (7)

4 Our hotel room had a lovely .... where we could sit out and see the sea. (7)

6 I have too many clothes to fit in that small .... (8)

7 Don't put your hand on the .... It's still hot. (6)

8 I filled the .... with warm water and got in. (4)

10 He ran down the .... and almost fell. (6)

12 My grandmother has a lovely old .... of drawers where she keeps everything. (5)

13 My favourite place in my house is my .... because I have all my things there. (7)

2 Exam candidates often make spelling mistakes. <u>Underline</u> the mistakes in the sentences and correct them.

1 In my bedroom I have a bed, a desk, a cupbord and a wardrobe.

2 The furnature in my grandma's house is made by hand.

3 In the hall we've got a large mirrow on the wall.

4 We don't have a dinning room in our new flat.

5 Under the window there's a wooden chest of draws.

6 There's a small kitchin in my house which I share with three other people.

3 Choose the correct option in *italics*.

1 I've got an important exam *on / in* Thursday morning.

2 Shall we meet *on / at* the station this afternoon?

3 We heard the news on the radio *at / in* breakfast time.

4 There were no more chairs, so had to sit *on / in* the floor.

5 I waited *on / at* the bus stop, but the bus didn't come.

6 We went swimming *in / at* the sea.

2 Vocabulary extra

At school

1 Complete the crossword.

Across

1 If you want to learn photography, you could take a .... at the local college. (6)

2 Ellie's studying for a history .... at Durham University. (6)

4 You'll have to work really hard if you want a good .... in the test. (4)

5 I enjoy learning about the climate and countries, so I'd like to study .... at university. (9)

7 On Saturdays Adam goes to .... classes. At the moment he's learning how to use oil paints. (3)

8 Maths is a .... you either love or hate. (7)

10 This year we have to do a .... at school to promote recycling. Part of it is making a video. (7)

Down

1 The best part of studying .... is when we do experiments with chemicals in the lab. (9)

3 Most people need to learn a foreign .... if they want to live abroad. (8)

6 Amelia is the best .... in the class. She always gets good grades. (5)

9 Before the winter holidays we had PE once a week, but this .... we are going to have it twice.

2 Write the past simple form of these verbs.

1 do ....
2 fail ....
3 go ....
4 learn ....
5 pass ....
6 take ....
7 make ....
8 miss ....
9 pay ....
10 set off ....
11 study ....
12 teach ....

3 Complete the sentences with the correct form of the verbs in Exercise 2 in the past simple or present simple.

1 After I finish school I always .... home by bus and eat something before I .... my homework.

2 Last month all the students in Year 9 .... an important exam. Most of us .... so we don't have to study in the summer holidays.

3 Yesterday I .... for school at 7 o'clock but the bus was late so I .... the beginning of my maths class.

4 Although I .... all night for the exam last week, I .... because I was too tired to concentrate.

5 In Year 1 I .... to read and write and the teachers .... us basic maths as well.

6 When the teacher talks in history class we .... notes and always .... attention.

4 Correct the underlined mistakes in the sentences.

1 I'd like a job where I <u>do</u> a lot of money.
   ....

2 We all <u>make</u> fun when we go out at the weekends.
   ....

3 I like to <u>pass</u> the afternoon with my family.
   ....

4 My teacher <u>learned</u> me a lot of useful things last year.
   ....

5 My brother <u>made</u> his driving test yesterday but I don't know if he passed.
   ....

6 You were late this morning. Did you <u>lose</u> the bus?
   ....

3 Vocabulary extra

Having fun

1 Complete the sentences with words from the box.

> bake   board   brush   cameras   chain   digital
> fire   helmet   performance   practise   queen   recipe
> sleeping bag   water   watercolours   wetsuit

1 I fell off my bike when the .... broke but luckily I was wearing a ....
2 I sometimes .... a cake without following a .... as an experiment. It usually tastes good!
3 I like to use a thin .... when I paint with ....
4 Although it was cold, we were comfortable by the .... but I was happy I had a good .... once we got in the tent.
5 Of course I only take .... photos. The old-fashioned .... are too expensive and more complicated to use.
6 I have to .... every day for hours before I give a public ....
7 I moved my .... to the square in the corner of the .... and then I realised that was not a good move.
8 I love the silence under the .... and I have a special .... to keep me warm.

2 Now match the sentences in Exercise 1 to the activities A–H.

A camping ....
B diving ....
C playing the piano ....
D photography ....
E playing chess ....
F cooking ....
G cycling ....
H painting ....

3 Complete the dialogues with a verb from the box. Sometimes more than one answer is possible.

> afford   enjoy   fancy   feel like   finish
> go off   look forward to   promise   put down
> remember   run out of   suggest   take

1 **A:** I've got a headache so I don't .... going to the cinema tonight.
   B: Never mind. I'll .... going when you are better.
2 **A:** What do you think I should do to relax?
   B: I .... doing yoga. It certainly makes me feel calm.
3 **A:** My old camera doesn't .... very good photos.
   B: Can't you .... to buy a new one? Why don't you look in the sale?
4 **A:** You must .... to buy some bread today.
   B: OK. I .... to do it on my way home from work.
5 **A:** When you go to the shops, can you get me a pen? Mine is going to .... ink.
   B: OK! I'll do it after I .... cleaning the car.
6 **A:** I .... going skiing again this winter.
   B: Really? I thought you would .... the idea of skiing after your accident last year.
7 **A:** I want to .... my name .... for the school basketball team this year.
   B: Good idea! I'm sure you'll .... playing.

On holiday

1 Complete the email with words or phrases from the box.

> dry   good time   hang   hire   journey   market
> original   peace and quiet   sightseeing
> snorkelling   souvenirs   trip

Hi Eva,

How's the summer going? We're having a
(1) .... here in Cancún, Mexico. The weather
is warm but wet because it's the rainy season. We go out
in T-shirts but it rains every day so it's difficult to stay
(2) .... It doesn't matter, it's not cold!

There are things for all the family to do here. On Monday we
decided to **(3)** .... bikes and we cycled along
the coast. My sister wanted to go **(4)** ....
yesterday, so I went with her and we saw some amazing
fish. My mum and dad decided they wanted some
(5) .... , so they stayed in the hotel, reading
by the pool.

Tomorrow the hotel has organised a **(6)** ....
to see some pyramids, so we're planning to go
(7) .... there and also visit a town where
we can look around a street **(8)** .... and
go shopping. Maybe I'll buy some **(9)** ....
I'll get you something **(10)** .... , not just a
T-shirt! The only bad thing is the **(11)** ....
home – sixteen hours in a plane is exhausting.

I hope you're having a good holiday too and get to
(12) .... out with friends and do fun things.

Lots of love,

Freddie

2 Complete the crossword.

Across

3 Kings and queens sometimes live in this beautiful building. (6)

5 Local people can go to the town .... to talk to somebody official about their neighbourhood. (4)

8 An example of this could be a statue of a king or an important building. (8)

9 Going on a .... is a great way to see lots of different places. (6)

10 My friends and I go to the .... club every Saturday to play table tennis or table football. (5)

11 I love .... I enjoy sleeping in a tent. (7)

Down

1 There's lots you can do in the .... centre: swim, go to the gym and use the climbing wall. (6)

2 I had to go up to the fourth floor of the .... store to find shoes and bags. (10)

4 In an art .... you can see wonderful paintings and special exhibitions. (7)

6 There are noisy machines in this place so all the .... workers wear ear protection. (7)

7 There's a beautiful one in the town square – they turn on the water three times a day. (8)

5 Vocabulary extra

Different feelings

1 Match the emojis to the feelings.

> annoyed   cheerful   confused   embarrassed
> frightened   jealous   miserable   surprised

1

2

3

4

....

5

6

7

8

....

2 Complete the table with adjectives from the box.

> afraid   angry   ashamed   bored   brave   cute
> depressed   disappointed   funny   generous
> grateful   guilty   pleased   satisfied

Positive adjectives	Negative adjectives

3 Complete the sentences with an adjective from Exercise 2. If necessary, change the form of the adjective from *-ed* to *-ing*.

1 I think the news on TV is really .... The reporters say nothing interesting.
2 My dad brought home a .... puppy last week. It looks like a little ball of fur.
3 I was really .... when my sister broke my phone. I shouted at her.
4 I ate the last biscuit and then I felt .... because my little brother was hungry.
5 My uncle always invites the whole family to have lunch in a restaurant on his birthday. He's very ....
6 Ellie was .... when the stranger gave her the money she had dropped in the street.
7 I think he's .... to swim in the sea in winter.
8 Scoring the winning goal in a match is very ....

4 Choose the correct option in *italics*.

1 I had a very *tired / tiring* day shopping today.
2 Eva was really *surprised / surprising* when she got the message.
3 I love horror movies or series that are *frightened / frightening*.
4 After work I like to listen to *relaxing / relaxed* music.
5 I was *amazed / amazing* when I managed to beat my brother at tennis.
6 His message was very *confused / confusing*, so I didn't know what to do.

5 Complete the sentences with a preposition.

1 The whole class is crazy .... the new video game.
2 You shouldn't be afraid .... that bully.
3 I feel nervous .... speaking in public.
4 My sister was very pleased .... her new phone.
5 Jake was embarrassed .... his old clothes.
6 You must be very proud .... your son getting such a good job.

6 Vocabulary extra

That's entertainment!

1 Complete the crossword.

Across

1 My sister went to the comic .... in Barcelona to see all the new Japanese magazines and characters. (4)

7 After the first half of the concert there was an .... so we went to the café. (8)

9 The cinema is sometimes called the big .... (6)

11 Steven Spielberg is a well-known film .... (8)

12 Cartoons are my favourite type of .... (9)

Down

2 I want to be an actor because I love performing in front of an .... (8)

3 .... to the museum is £5 for adults and £2 for children. (9)

4 Actors stand on the .... to perform in a theatre. (5)

5 After a performance, journalists sometimes write a .... to give their opinion. (6)

6 I love the TV .... about a hospital and the people who work there. (6)

8 The play is very popular so you have to .... tickets early. (4)

10 We sat in the front .... of the theatre so we could see the actors perfectly. (3)

2 Choose the correct option in *italics*.

1 Have you ever seen your favourite singer perform *live / alive*?

2 The actor appeared on a *chat / reality* show yesterday to talk about her new film and her life.

3 I like classical music and singing, so I enjoy going to the *opera / musical*.

4 The *crowd / audience* at the football match went crazy when their team scored a goal.

5 I helped to make the *scenery / tickets* for the school play by painting trees and flowers.

6 My mum really loves dancing so we go to the *ballet / circus* once a year.

3 Complete the sentences with words from the box.

> been   found out   gone   got to know
> known   met

1 I've .... how to get cheap tickets for the concert. A friend of mine works with the band.

2 Jessie has .... to Germany for the whole summer. She won't be back until September.

3 Have you ever .... a famous footballer in real life?

4 We've .... our neighbours for many years.

5 I really like Katie now I've .... her better. I thought she was a bit strange at first.

6 Danny's .... to America several times because he has an uncle there.

Getting around

1 Match the words from box A with the words from box B to make compound words. Then label the photos with the compound words.

....

....

....

A

car   rail   round   thunder   traffic   under

B

about   ground   jam   park   storms   way

2 Complete the sentences with a compound word from Exercise 1.

1 You shouldn't walk over the ....
because there are too many cars going round it.

2 I prefer to travel by .... in a big city because it's faster than the bus.

3 Take the train and I'll meet you outside the
.... station.

4 I don't mind .... but I'm afraid of lightning.

5 You can always find a space in the big
.... at the supermarket.

6 We were late because there was a huge
.... in the city centre because of the football match.

3 Complete the holiday blog with the sentences below. Write A–E in the gaps.

Can the weather spoil a holiday?

Read our readers' comments

Mick: You can't always expect the weather to be fine here in June. Most of the time **(1)** .... Still, we had umbrellas and it was good not to be sightseeing in the heat.

Rebecca: I wanted to climb the mountain but there was a huge storm. Although **(2)** .... , I watched from the safety of my room.

Louis: Our plan was to go to the coast and walk along the beach to see the birds and watch people sailing, but that day **(3)** .... , and we couldn't see more than two metres in front of us.

Anna: The best part of the trip was when **(4)** .... so we could go skating on the lake. It was very cold but we wore warm clothes and had a lot of fun.

Finley: Although the forecast said it was going to be cold and wet, in fact **(5)** .... nearly the whole time we were there, so we went to the beach every day.

A the temperature was below freezing

B the sky was cloudy and there were showers

C it was warm and dry

D the thunder and lightning were really impressive

E it was really foggy

8 Vocabulary extra

Influencers

1 Match the opposites.

1	miserable	**a**	hard-working
2	modern	**b**	rude
3	lazy	**c**	smart
4	stupid	**d**	quiet
5	noisy	**e**	old-fashioned
6	polite	**f**	cheerful

2 Complete the sentences with words from Exercise 1.

1 They are always talking loudly. They are ....
2 Carmen walked along the road smiling and singing to herself. She was ....
3 I want a phone that uses the latest technology. I want a .... phone.
4 Elly never does her homework. She is ....
5 Her shoes look like the ones my mother wore when she was young. They are ....
6 Hugo always says 'please' and 'thank you'. He is ....
7 Henry looks really unhappy. He is ....
8 They tried to push to the front of the queue. They were ....

3 Complete the word puzzle and find the word in grey.

1 She doesn't worry about giving presentations. She is ....
2 He always shares the snacks he brings to school. He is ....
3 She never offers to help anyone. She is ....
4 She doesn't say much. She's very ....
5 He worries a lot about problems. He is ....
6 They always help their neighbours. They are ....
7 He doesn't like to talk in public. He is ....

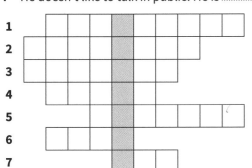

4 Answer the questions about Danny, Jamie, Olivia and Sara.

1 Who has got a moustache? ....
2 What is Olivia's hair like? .... , ...
   and ....
3 Who has got a scar? ....
4 Who has got broad shoulders? ....
5 What is Danny's hair like? .... and
   ....
6 What is Sara's hair like? .... and
   ....
7 Who is slim? .... and ....
8 Who is bald? ....

5 Choose the correct option in *italics*.

1 Caitlin was late to school because she didn't hear her alarm, but she *made up / found out* an excuse that the bus didn't come.
2 I spent my childhood in the countryside, where I *brought up / grew up* on a farm.
3 My best friend and I didn't *take up / get on* very well with each other when we were younger, but now we are always together.
4 Harry wanted to have his own business but he *ran out of / set up* money after a few months and had to close the company.

Stay fit and healthy

1 Complete the sentences with one or two words.

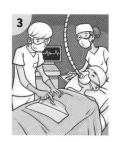

1 He's .... finger.
2 She's got a ....
3 He's having an ....
4 She's taking some ....
5 He's got a .... on his arm.
6 She's putting a .... on his wound.

2 Choose the correct option in *italics*.

1 I used to *go / play / have* swimming every day when I was younger.
2 The athletes couldn't run because the *pitch / court / track* was too wet.
3 We *hit / drew / scored* in the final thirty seconds and won the match!
4 There is a badminton *court / pitch / match* at my local sports centre where we can practise.
5 My brother *did / went / made* skiing last winter.
6 The golfer *kicked / hit / threw* the ball 200m.
7 Do you often *practise / do / go* sport?
8 She likes to go to yoga classes in the *stadium / gym / court* once a week.
9 We play soccer on an artificial *track / pitch / court* at school.
10 If you try hard, I'm sure you'll *win / beat / draw* the other team.

3 Match the words in the box with the pictures. Write down a sport that uses each type of equipment.

| bat   gloves   helmet   kit   net   racket |
| swimsuit   trainers |

1 *helmet — cycling, ice hockey, American football*
2 ....
3 ....
4 ....
5 ....
6 ....
7 ....
8 ....

10 Vocabulary extra

Looks amazing!

1 Complete the crossword.

Across

2 the person who buys something in a shop (8)
4 A dentist looks after your .... (5)
5 You can study or read books here. (7)
7 You can buy cakes or bread here. (6)
10 This person will cut or dye your hair. (11)
11 a piece of paper that shows how much you have to pay (4)

Down

1 something you buy at a reduced price (7)
3 a person who doesn't eat meat (10)
6 a person who sells meat (7)
8 a person who sells medicine (7)
9 a place where you have your car repaired (6)

2 Choose the correct option in *italics*.

1 I had my broken phone *mended / reserved*.
2 Can we *borrow / lend* a tent for the camping trip?
3 I *caught / complained* to the manager about the meal.
4 Chloe *did / made* an appointment at the hairdresser's.
5 You'll need to *book / hire* a room for your holiday soon.

3 Put the food words in the correct category. Some words belong to more than one category.

> beef   bread   butter   cake   cheese   chicken
> chips   chocolate   cucumber   eggs   grapes
> lettuce   pasta   pear   rice
> steak   sweets   tuna   yoghurt

Proteins	Carbohydrates	Fruit & vegetables	Dairy products	Fats & sugars

4 Match the words to the pictures.

> chopsticks   fork   frying pan   glass   jug   knife
> plate   spoon

....

....

The natural world

1 Label the pictures with the words in the box.

> beach   cliff   hill   island   lake   rock   stream
> valley   waterfall   wood

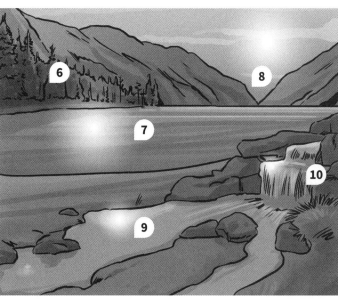

2 Choose the correct option in *italics*.

1 Many people in big cities have health problems because of the *prevention / pollution* caused by cars.
2 An alternative energy source could be *solar / sun* power.
3 If we build more houses in the countryside, the *live / wild* animals will lose their habitat.
4 Reusing objects for different purposes helps reduce *weight / waste*.
5 Governments create national parks to *protect / preven* animals.
6 Tigers are in *danger / worry* of extinction.
7 You should give up having baths to *keep / save* water.
8 One of the *aims / finals* of the project is to create more green areas in the city.

3 Complete the text with words from the box and the correct suffix: *-ation, -ion* or *-ment*.

> announce   create   discuss   educate   enjoy
> excite   invite   reduce

1 April

The **(1)** .... that was made last week by the President has surprised many teachers and students. She stated that after a long
(2) .... the government has decided to replace all course books with tablets. The
(3) .... of new online material will be the responsibility of local authorities. This news has caused great **(4)** .... among students and it is certain that the **(5)** .... they will get from using the new technology will benefit their learning because they will also have fun. Some teachers have already received an
(6) .... to attend training courses and most of them are pleased with the change to the
(7) .... system. The
(8) .... in paper needed for books will also help the environment.

12 Vocabulary extra

Express yourself!

1 Choose the correct option in *italics*.

1 Megan often tells *lies / jokes / messages* about why she is late for class and the teacher never believes her.

2 We will send you *a letter / an email / a selfie* in the next thirty seconds to confirm your registration on the course.

3 You need to ask *to your parents / for your parents / your parents* if you can go on the trip.

4 When I was younger, I couldn't *say / speak / talk* any French, but now I know a lot.

5 I'm not sure of the *vocabulary / communication / meaning* of the word 'geek'.

6 My brother went to the USA and learnt lots of *slang / chats / translations* from his friends, like the word 'sweet', which means 'nice' or 'good'.

7 When you want to go, please *say / tell / speak* goodbye to your grandma.

8 If you need anything, *say / speak / ask* the shop assistant for help.

2 Match the beginnings and endings of these sentences.

1 You'll need a password to

2 If you receive a strange email,

3 I haven't got enough space on my phone to

4 There are several film blogs where you can

5 It's not a good idea to give any personal information when you

6 Choose the correct option and

7 It's an online form, so you don't need to

8 You can use an emoji to show your feelings when you

a drag it to the space provided.

b print anything.

c connect to the internet in this café.

d post your comments.

e send messages.

f delete it immediately.

g install that app.

h chat online.

3 Complete the sentences with a word from the box. Use a negative prefix where necessary.

> complete   expensive   fair   healthy   patient
> perfect   polite   successful

1 Eating too many sweet things is ....

2 You have to be .... when waiting at the doctor's.

3 It was .... to give him extra work when he had done nothing wrong.

4 It's important to be .... when you talk to older people.

5 I've just started playing tennis, so I don't need an .... racket.

6 Daniel went for a job interview but he was .... , so he'll have to try harder next time.

7 You can't be right all the time. Nobody is ....

8 The story was .... because it didn't have an ending.

Acknowledgements

The authors and publishers acknowledge the following sources of copyright material and are grateful for the permissions granted. While every effort has been made, it has not always been possible to identify the sources of all the material used, or to trace all copyright holders. If any omissions are brought to our notice, we will be happy to include the appropriate acknowledgements on reprinting and in the next update to the digital edition, as applicable.

Key: U = Unit

Text

U3: Megan Knowles-Bacon for the text and listening material. Reproduced with kind permission of Megan Knowles-Bacon; **U8**: Mikaila Ulmer for the text and listening material. Copyright © Mikaila Ulmer. Reproduced with permission of D'Andra Ulmer; **U11**: Magnus Henneberger for the text about Magnus Henneberger. Reproduced with kind permission of Jill Henneberger.

Photography

The following images are sourced from Getty Images.
U1: Hero Images; master1305/iStock/Getty Images Plus; Anthony Asael/Art in All of Us/Corbis News; John Greim/Photolibrary; gloriasalgado/RooM; **U2**: Peter Muller/Cultura; Vesna Jovanovic/EyeEm; monkeybusinessimages/iStock/Getty Images Plus; Radius Images/Getty Images Plus; **U3**: leaf/iStock/Getty Images Plus; valentinrussanov/E+; Ascent Xmedia/The Image Bank; **U4**: Cultura RM Exclusive/Gary John Norman; Bernd Vogel/Corbis; Atlantide Phototravel/Corbis Documentary; cinoby/iStock/Getty Images Plus; **U5**: Sidekick/iStock/Getty Images Plus; apomares/E+; Steve Debenport/E+; Stanton j Stephens/Image Source; **U6**: Hill Street Studios/Blend Images; Burak Karademir/Moment; SolStock/E+; dmbaker/iStock/Getty Images Plus; VikramRaghuvanshi/iStock/Getty Images Plus; Dimitri Otis/Photographer's Choice; PeopleImages/E+; **U7**: fotog; Simon Marcus Taplin/Corbis; FokinOl/iStock/Getty Images Plus; Steve Debenport/E+; Gail Shotlander/Moment; Boris Jordan Photography/Moment; fotog; chictype/iStock/Getty Images Plus; Hans Blossey/imageBROKER; Chris Hellier/Corbis Documentary; **U8**: Jupiterimages/Stockbyte; Ada Summer/Corbis; Westend61; Compassionate Eye Foundation/DigitalVision; ByeByeTokyo/E+; amriphoto/E+; Sven Hansche/EyeEm; J. Kempin/Getty Images Entertainment; Simon Gardner/First Light; **U9**: svetikd/E+; ImageDB/iStock/Getty Images Plus; mbbirdy/iStock Unreleased; Manuel-F-O/iStock/Getty Images Plus; imagenavi; pic_studio/iStock/Getty Images Plus; InterestingLight/iStock/Getty Images Plus; Alex Ortega/EyeEm; supermimicry/iStock Unreleased; Brent Winebrenner/Lonely Planet Images; Jordan Mansfield/Stringer/Getty Images Sport; Peter Dazeley/Photographer's Choice; Stephen Oliver/Dorling Kindersley; Westend61; Kameleon007/iStock/Getty Images Plus; talevr/iStock/Getty Images Plus; rolleiflextlr/iStock/Getty Images Plus; Creative Crop/Photodisc; Vevchic86/iStock/Getty Images Plus; **U10**: drbimages/iStock/Getty Images Plus; shanghaiface/Moment; Flashpop/Iconica; Ranta Images/iStock/Getty Images Plus; Yuri_Arcurs/DigitalVision; JGI/Jamie Grill/Blend Images; **U11**: apomares/iStock/Getty Images Plus; Moment; Nigel Pavitt/AWL Images; Robert Daly/Caiaimage; **U12**: Sebastian Pfuetze/Taxi; Sofia Apkalikov/Moment Open; Caiaimage/Paul Bradbury; jamtoons/DigitalVision Vectors.

The following photographs have been sourced from other sources.
U3: © Mark Hesketh-Jennings/Megan Knowles-Bacon; **U9**: © Mikaila Ulmer.

Front cover photography by Tetra Images - Erik Isakson/Brand X Pictures/Getty Images; Xinzheng/Moment/Getty Images.

Illustrations

Amerigo Pinelli and Abel Ippolito

Audio

Produced by Leon Chambers and recorded at The SoundHouse Studios, London

Page make up

Wild Apple Design Ltd